HENRIK IBSEN

was born of well-to-do parents at Skien, a small Norwegian coastal town, on March 20, 1828. In 1836 his father went bankrupt, and the family was reduced to near poverty. At the age of fifteen, he was apprenticed to an apothecary in Grimstad. In 1850 Ibsen went to Christiania—present-day Oslo—as a student, with the hope of becoming a doctor. On the strength of his first two plays, he was appointed "theater-poet" to the new Bergen National Theater, where he wrote five conventional romantic and historical dramas and absorbed the elements of his craft. In 1857 he was called to the director-ship of the financially unsound Christiania Norwegian Theater, which failed in 1862. In 1864, exhausted and enraged by the frustration of his efforts toward a national drama and theater, he quit Norway for what became twenty-seven years of volun-tary exile abroad. In Italy he wrote the volcanic *Brand* (1866), which made his reputation and secured him a poet's stipend from the government. Its companion piece, the phantasma-goric *Peer Gynt*, followed in 1867, then the immense double play, *Emperor and Galilean* (1873), expressing his philosophy of civilization. Meanwhile, having moved to Germany, Ibsen had been searching for a new style. With *The Pillars of Society* he found it; this became the first of twelve plays, appearing at two-year intervals, that confirmed his international stand-ing as the foremost dramatist of his age. In 1900 Ibsen suf-fered the first of several strokes that incapacitated him. He died in Oslo on May 23, 1906.

HENRIK IBSEN

PEER GYNT
A Dramatic Poem

A New Translation with a Foreword
by ROLF FJELDE

A SIGNET CLASSIC
PUBLISHED BY THE NEW AMERICAN LIBRARY

First Printing, March, 1964

SIGNET TRADEMARK REG. U.S. PAT. OFF. AND FOREIGN COUNTRIES
REGISTERED TRADEMARK—MARCA REGISTRADA
HECHO EN CHICAGO, U.S.A.

NOV '64 WI

SIGNET CLASSICS *are published by*
The New American Library of World Literature, Inc.
501 Madison Avenue, New York, New York 10022

PRINTED IN THE UNITED STATES OF AMERICA

TO MY

MOTHER AND FATHER

for the inborn note, the star

FOREWORD

> To have a self, to be a self, is the greatest concession made to man, but at the same time it is eternity's demand upon him.
>
> KIERKEGAARD

In the spring of 1864, like countless other artists seeking a thaw of feeling and a renewal of hope, Henrik Ibsen passed for the first time through that towering continental rock barrier that separates two climates, two outlooks and two antiquities. What this transition meant to him, he could still remember clearly in a speech given thirty-four years later: "Upon the vast mountains hung clouds like great dark curtains, and underneath them we drove through tunnels, finding ourselves suddenly at Miramare, where the beauty of the South, a wonderful soft brightness, shining like white marble, was suddenly revealed to me and was destined to set its stamp on all my later production, even if that production was not all beauty."

For Ibsen the Alps were to separate more than the Gothic North from the Mediterranean South, though he could hardly have known it at the time. He had just turned thirty-six. Behind him were ten plays, most of which had failed in performance, some several dozen poems, a scattering of newspaper pieces and speculative papers on literary subjects. Behind him, also, lay Norway, which meant a proud, dead viking past and some of the most spectacular and legend-haunted scenery in

Europe, but more importantly and immediately, memories of the bankruptcy of his father, social ostracism, grinding poverty in cheerless, wintry towns, a hard apprenticeship at the Bergen Theater, debts, unproductive overwork as a theater director, bankruptcy again, more debts, the recognition and preferment of less gifted contemporaries, contrasted with his own customary reception in the press ("Herr Ibsen as a dramatic author is a complete nonentity"). There were a few bright spots—most recently, a modest government travel grant—but the view to the north was largely dark. Ahead to the south lay Italy and, unforseeably within three years, two of his greatest plays, hinged like a diptych on one event, the dramatic poems *Brand* and *Peer Gynt*.

That event was the brief Prusso-Danish War, then at its height. The duchies of Schleswig and Holstein, strategically situated at the neck of the Jutland peninsula between Denmark and Prussia, had for years been a focus of tension between those countries. Schleswig traditionally and, with less justification, ethnically had long been considered a fief of the Danish crown, and this status had lately been confirmed by treaty. In 1862, however, Bismarck became chancellor of Prussia; and along with his vision of German unification and his maxim that "the great questions of our time will be settled by blood and iron," he held other views on the Schleswig-Holstein controversy. "From the beginning," he wrote, "I kept annexation steadily before my eyes." When, in March 1863, King Frederick III issued a royal proclamation unequivocally making Schleswig Danish soil, the incipient crisis came to a head.

The policy that advocated closer ties between Denmark, Sweden, and Norway and common action in the face of an external threat went by the name of Scandinavianism. It was fervently championed among the students and young professionals; in December 1863, as the Prussian invasion was being mounted, the Christiania students' club passed a resolution vowing to take up arms for their "brothers" on the Danish frontier. Joint action, on the other hand, was opposed by the peasants, particularly in the rural areas of Sweden and Norway, who feared Russian expansion more than Prussia and hoped, by standing pat, to give offense to no one. For the history of world drama, Scandinavianism has its major importance as the one article of political faith that Ibsen consistently upheld throughout his lifetime.

Thus, when the newly reorganized and expanded Prussian army, dieted on Clausewitz and led by Moltke, invaded Schleswig in February 1864 and swept victoriously northward into Denmark, Scandinavianism and Ibsen's ideals were simultaneously put to the test. As Bismarck had so shrewdly foreseen and prepared through his manipulations, none of the great powers came to Denmark's aid. Charles XV of the dual kingdom of Sweden-Norway prudently opted for nonintervention. As Ibsen, traveling southward toward Italy, reached Berlin, he could see the cannon from the Danish forts at Dybbøl, those cannon that had fired without relief until they burst, hauled into the capital amid shouts of triumph, and he watched the crowds spit into the muzzles of the guns. "To me," he wrote, "it was a sign of how history someday will spit into the eyes of Norway and Sweden for the sake of this affair."

The outraged sense of personal betrayal that Ibsen felt was twofold. First, through the isolation and defeat of Denmark, Scandinavianism had been vitiated; and this cause Ibsen had made particularly and powerfully his own. It was the contemporary implication of his most recent play, *The Pretenders,* in which the conflict between King Haakon and Earl Skule revolves around the analogous national consolidation of thirteenth-century Norway. Secondly, his ideals, based on inwardly evolving and as yet largely unarticulated insights into the laws of human nature, had been betrayed, so to speak, in the impotence of their childhood, much like the threadball thoughts that roll accusingly after Peer Gynt. Norway, since the Napoleonic Wars, had been joined to the Swedish crown as the inferior, backward partner; Ibsen's ideals therefore decreed that his country be "absolutely and in every respect independent." As with individuals, so with nations, there could be no true union except between equals. What credible reason was there for building up a national theater and a new dramaturgy, other than to strengthen the people by reminding them of their past best selves and teaching them to "think greatly." The Danish crisis had been an opportunity for Norway now to *act* greatly and with strength. Instead, noninvolvement was nothing more than self-defeat, something Ibsen could readily identify with his own sense of helpless rage.

And yet, in this coming together of roles and feelings, by that mysterious law in art and life which he had already affirmed in himself, that law whereby much must be suffered before much can be given, one can see that Ibsen had gained inestimably. Following the precedent of his first serious modern play, *Love's Comedy*, two years before, he renounced once and for all the romantic twilight of the Eddas and the sagas. His work entered the history of his time, and he began to speak, not for an aesthetic program or an archaic dream, but for a nation, a people, and an age. Without this deepening and transforming connection to a larger life, Brand and Peer Gynt could never have emerged the archetypal figures that they are.

But the transformation did not occur instantaneously; it came about, as was characteristic with Ibsen, gradually, over many months, after false starts and hard struggle. First he merely subsided into the liberating experience of Italy. After two initial weeks in Rome, he moved out to Genzano in the Alban Hills for the summer. A stocky, genial figure with a short black beard and a broad-brimmed hat that gave him the name "Cappellone" among the townspeople, he spent his afternoons reading or exploring the countryside. In the evenings there were tours with friends around the Lake of Nemi. In the mornings he worked. His original intention had been to write a historical drama in five acts on the life of the Faroe pirate Magnus Heinesen; this, however, would only have been another of those costumed glorifications of the past that camouflaged the poverty of the present. He abandoned this idea and talked of writing a play about Julian the Apostate, reaching further back in history to the divided roots of Western civilization, the divergent ideals of paganism and Christianity. But in actuality he had already begun a long narrative poem about a fanatical country pastor locked in conflict with himself, his congregation, his mission, and his God. The protagonist's name was Koll, meaning "mountain peak," but presently he changed it to Brand, with its dual connotation of "fire" and "sword."

When he returned in the fall to Rome, joined there by his wife and small son, he felt he had found a second home in Italy. It was a year, however, before the new environment completed its work of liberation. The following July, living now largely on the dole of friends in Christiania, Ibsen threw away a whole year's effort and began again, casting his lot—for the rest of his life, as it proved—with the dramatic form. Writing long hours at an inspired pace, he had, in three months' time, the finished draft of a play whose power and scope were unprecedented in his former production or, for that matter, in the entire theater of the northern countries; when it appeared in March 1866, it won immediate acceptance throughout Scandinavia and ran through three large editions by the year's end. The ebb tide of defeat at last had turned.

"After *Brand*," Ibsen wrote, "*Peer Gynt* followed almost as of itself." In the earlier play, the God-intoxicated protagonist descends from the mountains, bringing the ruthless claims of the absolute down to the hearts of the villagers, forcing sacrifices first on his family, then on his congregation, inspiring them, goading them beyond themselves into building a new church to mark a new life, then repudiating this temple of idolatry to lead them out in the open, back up the mountain to worship freely in spirit and truth, until they lose faith, turn on him, stone him, and leave him to press on, like incarnate will itself, up to the ice-church to die in an avalanche alone. In shaping the tragedy of this Savonarola of the fjords, Ibsen's mind must have played with the possibility of creating his counterpart, the man with no ruling passion, no calling, no commitment, the eternal opportunist, the mirror of surfaces, the charming, gifted, self-centered child who turns out finally to have neither center nor self. After *Brand* was published and its success assured, he had both the buoyancy and the means to attempt it, and he proceeded rapidly to the composition of what, for many, remains the richest and greatest of his works.

Following a summer at Frascati, largely spent wrestling in vain with material for the play about the Emperor Julian, he returned to Rome. During the dark days of the writing of *Brand,* he had read nothing but the Bible; now he immersed himself in the broad humor and sparkling phrases of the eighteenth-century Danish playwright Ludvig Holberg, the "Molière of the North," born in Bergen, where his own initiation in theater had occurred. At the beginning of November, a letter to his publisher indicates that new subjects were stirring in him. By New Year's of 1867, he was hard at work on notes and a scenario for a dramatic poem about "one of the half mythical, romantic characters out of Norwegian folklore of recent times." Ibsen's confidence in his new conception is clearly apparent in the fact that, by early August, he could send the first three acts direct to press from his summer quarters on the island of Ischia. A few days later a slight earthquake disturbed his productive stay on the island; he promptly moved to Sorrento, where the last two acts were written and mailed off within two months. On November 14, 1867, *Peer Gynt* was published by Gyldendal in Copenhagen, and the diptych was complete.

The actual historical prototype for the legendary character of Peer Gynt is still open to debate. Some authorities derive the name from one Peder Laurisen Günter, of a seventeenth-century German aristocratic family settled in Norway. A more appealing and suggestive derivation, in view of the trollish propensity for distorted vision, would identify the name with a Peder Olsen Hage, nicknamed Gynt, conjecturally from the root *gjyne,* "to see." We know that Ibsen, in any case, believed in his hero's authenticity. In 1862, aided by a university grant, he had taken a two-month walking tour from Christiania northward to Romsdal and Sunnmøre for the purpose of gathering folklore. From his findings at that time, he could report to his publisher that "Peer Gynt is a real person who lived in the Gudbrandsdal, probably at the end of the last, or the beginning of this century. His name is still well known among the people up there, but nothing particular is remembered of his doings, beyond what is to be found in Asbjørnsen's *Norwegian Fairy Tales.*"

The collections of popular tales by Asbjørnsen and Moe provide the single most important source of material for the play. In these, one finds not merely the original germ of the character Peer Gynt, but also Gudbrand Glesne's ride, the three farm girls, the Boyg, the Woman in Green, the eye operation of the trolls, the tale of the devil in the nut, the castles called Soria-Moria and East of the Sun and West of the Moon, and the talking threadballs. To these shards of folklore, Ibsen added his own observations of his more Gyntian contemporaries. Among others, the flamboyant virtuoso Ole Bull made his unwitting contribution, as did the poet and linguistic nationalist, A. O. Vinje, who was to be still more devastatingly satirized as the language reformer Huhu. Not least among these were traits of the peasant class at large, sentimentally portrayed in most of the fiction of the time, but to Ibsen's mind the chief betrayers of Scandinavian unity and therefore, like Peer, windy exponents of the promise for the deed.

What really matters, however, in all these circumstances of composition is how the imagination of the poet succeeds in penetrating through historical material to myth, to the form of the irreducible event. In the characters and actions of his major plays, Ibsen always gives us three things: the sometimes obscure, sometimes well-documented inflections of his inward and outward biography at a given historic moment; the progressive psychological revelations of roles, characterizations, human destinies that live independently on the page and in the actor's art; and behind these individual figures, gigantic and mysterious principles that move, interact, and develop out of the hidden depths of life. We can learn by studying the first and by perceptively appreciating the second, but we can never afford to lose sight of the last, for these are what give Ibsen's theater, which often seems on the surface so confined, its peculiar resonance and strength. In *Peer Gynt,* as nowhere else, we have the sense of ulterior forces brought up from a usually buried awareness, as if the whole action of the play took place with the top layers of the mind peeled off.

To show, in anything like its full complexity of pattern and meaning, the archetype at work behind the personae of the actual in an Ibsen play would involve a commentary far too lengthy for this introduction. One can perhaps suggest some part of its over-all structuring power, however, by focusing briefly on several aspects of the total design of *Peer Gynt,* namely, the opposing figures of Solveig and the trolls, the fate of the draft-evading farm boy, and the significant repetitions-with-variation in Act Four of motifs from Peer's youth.

It is no accident that Peer Gynt encounters both Solveig and the trolls within two or three days of each other. Peer, as we meet him at the opening of the play, is a powerfully built youth of twenty. His experience of religion, we learn much later, has come to him in easy doses in his middle years. Thus, though he has lived to himself in his fantasies to a great extent, he has had no cause, either physical or spiritual, to examine his life. When he acts, he does so unreflectively and irresponsibly, going off during his mother's busiest time on the farm to hunt reindeer. He may be said, at this stage then, to represent existence without self-awareness, a state of harmonious union with nature. The emblem of this state is the ride on the reindeer's back, animal and man blended into one purposeless, blindly charging force. The course of the ride is down the dizzying razor's edge of unconditioned freedom, and the ride becomes, as it must, a leap and a fall. But it is the utter, intoxicating freedom, even of the fall, that stays with Peer ("Imagine —a reindeer, falling free—/With never the hard earth under me!") Imagine—yes; because no man can live that unconditioned freedom except in dreams or in the imaginative play of childhood.

What makes Peer obscurely but decisively aware of

his own existence, his own finite, yet marvelously potent—and potential—self is the encounter with Solveig. Their meeting, for him, is a true *ekstasis;* for the first time in his life, he comes poignantly and exaltedly outside himself. But to discover one's potentiality as a self-transcending being, no longer lapped in the mindless flow of nature and one's dreaming childhood, is also to discover the opposite, the potentiality of becoming less than oneself, of becoming, in other words, a troll.

What is it to be a troll? The genus is well described by M. C. Bradbrook when she speaks of a troll as being humanity minus the specifically human qualities. "The troll is the animal version of man, the alternative to man; he is also what man fears he may become." To reconstruct his origins in the Northern imagination, you need only take the train from Oslo through the Gudbrandsdal to Andalsnes. There, at the valley's upper end, in the pale green twilight of the brief summer night, the fjelds loom starkly black, abrupt, and menacing overhead, and to a sensitive eye, they may move slightly as you turn away. The genus troll comes out of these mountains and others like them. He is primeval and remorseless, permanent as rock in the nature of things. From another viewpoint, he may appear unreflective, irresponsible, purposeless—in other words, the animal that man remains if he fails to act upon his self-discovery. He exists, in fact, in the widest variety of forms. In our time he ran the death camps, and now maneuvers for kickbacks or mouths the tribal chant of nationalism. Instinctively he dislikes the open and gravitates toward caves, back rooms, closed thoughts and feelings. Yet with all his affinity for dark places, he shies away from the darkest place of all, himself. There he lives indolently on the surface, cutting corners, following fashions, getting by on compromise, accepting himself through custom and habit, rather than making the painful struggle to realize himself in truth and freedom. His mind, shapeless and indulgent at the core, is like a distorting prism; and with his passion for conformity, he must coerce all others to see things on his own bias. Above all, behind whatever disguise he wears, he finds his own ideas, his own prejudices, his own way of life, his clan, his class, his nation-state—enough. In the Ronde Mountains, we have him pure, but he exists, to some extent, in everyone.

The most impressive and formidable of all the trolls is that enveloping presence, that voice from the darkness, the Great Boyg. A rich symbol, suggestive of several interpretations, the Boyg receives one unmistakable definition within the play itself. In Act Four, Peer comes once again on what seems to be its likeness, in the shape of the Sphinx. We then recall that other self-made man who, centuries before, confronted and surmounted the crisis of the Sphinx. Significantly, now the roles are reversed. Oedipus was asked a riddle, and successfully responded. But here, Peer Gynt does the asking—and gets no response; the Sphinx is mute. If Peer were less the child of his age of unreason, he might see that the Sphinx is not there to be asked. It exists solely to be answered—with the commitment of one's whole being. And the answer, we remember, is "Man." To become man, to take on the total challenge of becoming human, is the only adequate reply to the riddle of the Sphinx.

The inducement for Peer to accept this challenge is, or ought to be, Solveig. Solveig is clearly no ordinary girl, a fact which considerably disturbs some critics. This patient Griselda who wastes herself in waiting is, they assert, hardly to be believed; how could she live out her years for so little? Such a judgment is founded on a too literal-minded realism. It is certainly true of most people that the bulk of their lives is a matter of bank statements and furniture bills, what to have for dinner and whether it rained all during vacation. But in *Peer Gynt,* Ibsen is not particularly interested in these surface levels of experience. Solveig is merely tangent to the everyday world; her real life is elsewhere. And that real life has to do with what she, as woman, has most to give. Approach Solveig as a naturalistic character, and she seems so far from ordinary as to be almost incredible; approach her as woman archetypally conceived, and she is not nearly so difficult to comprehend or portray.

In the over-all pattern of the play, Solveig is everything that the trolls are not. The trolls are the dark interior at the base of the mountain; she climbs to her proper home on the heights. The trolls drift and temporize; she stakes her life on one irrevocable choice. They go it alone, or at best join in an uneasy collective; she wants to share to the full. They are vindictive; she forgives. One of the things about her that troubles these same literalist critics is that, apart from some superficial signs of aging, she changes so little in the course of the play as to appear virtually static. But here I would trace Ibsen's meaning along the lines suggested by R. Ellis Roberts: that in Solveig's faith, her hope and her love is eternity's claim, from which she never departs. The real center of her life is in a timeless realm where love emanates and returns; and she participates in that timelessness. History, which fascinates Peer Gynt, we can be sure means nothing to her. World epochs rise and sweep to doom, thinkers perish and martyrs bleed, emperors wear their crowns of straw, while out of the waste spaces of the Sahara, out of the vast Egyptian night, where the stone idols wait, half-sunken like the wreck of Ozymandias in the sand, comes nothing but the endless blowing of the desert wind. Finding the truth in one human soul—for Ibsen, as for Shakespeare—outweighs all the pomps and casualties of time. Finding that truth is finally everything for Peer; making the discovery possible for one who, in her eyes, is a sufficient cause is finally everything for Solveig. How can she live for less?

With these two meetings then, the alternatives of the action are established, and Peer Gynt's life unrolls between them—the way of Solveig and the way of the troll. To be faced with alternatives implies the necessity of choice—and to choose so fundamentally, for Peer, is too difficult. The entire phantasmagoria of the play is the story of an unmade choice, the choice of being what you can become, namely, that nature-transcending, contradiction-torn, purpose-evolving, suffering, striving and achieving self which is truly man, and that spiritually anesthetized, fantasy-swathed, self-sufficing unborn thing which is a troll.

To become man is the underlying objective, the

Stanislavskian infinitive of the drama; but man, like the genus troll, is an abstraction, a universal, whereas truth for Ibsen never lies in the abstract, but in the specific, the individual confronted with the problematic concreteness of reality. What is it to become, not Man, but simply—or not so simply—*a* man. The question is raised and particularized in what deserves to be called the subplot of *Peer Gynt,* although unlike standard Shakespearean dramatic construction and that of other Ibsen plays such as *A Doll House,* it is stated within the strictest limits, being confined to no more than two scenes: the dumb show in Act Three, in which the farm boy amputates his finger, and the moving eulogy in Act Five, in which his life is summed up by the country pastor. Condensed as the presentation is, this other life must be thought of as moving invisibly parallel to Peer Gynt's own through the fifty-year span of the play, a silent and ironic commentary on its inauthentic character.

The parallelism is asserted by a number of points of correspondence. Both young men, of about the same age, stand separate from their communities. Both undergo a bitter initiation, the farm boy by running a gantlet of scorn, Peer Gynt by drinking the bowl of mead with the trolls. Each begets, in his own way, an illegitimate child. Each enters the world through a flight from responsibility and becomes as a result a cripple, the farm boy outwardly through his mutilated hand, Peer inwardly, as the Woman in Green observes, through being lame in his mind.

The similarities are clearly apparent, but so also are the contrasts. The farm boy's thoughts are restrained and tame; Peer's are impetuous and fantastic. The farm boy's voice lacks force; Peer's strength, Aase declares, is all in his mouth. The bearing of the anonymous youth lacks manliness; Peer makes a flagrant display of his virility with the three mountain girls. As much as these two are paralleled, they are contrasted; and it is the contrasts, ultimately, that dominate.

In a sense, then, the paired lives constitute two faces of the same coin, opposing profiles of the same persona. What differentiates them finally is less native endowment than choice, the choice made by the one and not by the other. And yet what delays and obviates the choice for Peer is nothing other than his most salient character trait, that tendency toward excessive fantasizing that Ibsen knew too well in his own life, that tendency that arises as a double-edged compensation out of a childhood such as Aase reveals during the search following the bride-rape. It is in this scene that Solveig suddenly understands, that she discerns, under the riot of Peer's ambitions, the boasting, the rage and self-centeredness, a human being groping to be born. She understands birth and children (Ibsen aptly gives her a little sister over whom she watches protectively at the wedding feast), and now she sees her work. At the end of the drama, Peer, to her, is still the groping child within the old, played-out, world-weary traveler.

What wearies Peer Gynt most is, in all his wandering, having missed so completely the springs of life; but his failure certainly stems in part from his mode of quest. Anyone who reads the text with some care is struck by the number of modulated repetitions of motifs from Peer's youth in the later action. His harsh treatment at the hands of the troll-imps, for example, is duplicated in his encounter with the Moroccan monkeys and again in the final chaos of the asylum scene. His invocation of the inviolable Anitra snoring in her tent repeats, in satiric reduction, his original refusal to approach Solveig in the hut. The enormous pig becomes the miraculous horse. He begins to quote the Bible, the classics, proverbs, acquaintances, himself, incessantly—and never quite accurately. The Memnon statue seems like the Dovre King; the Sphinx is like the Boyg.

In this mosaic of repeating patterns, Ibsen suggests that experience takes its shape primarily from the set of the personality, and that the world we never made is, often to a surprising extent, an outgrowth of our own human powers or a denial thereof, and not, as Peer passively claims, of Fate. But the repetitions, we also see, are veiled, disguised, off key, inaccurate; and in this fact are further implications. The Gyntian mode of procedure in all things, large or small, is roundabout. To go by roundabouts—or by the Rotation Method, to use the comparable term from *Either/Or*, one of the works of Kierkegaard read by Ibsen in his Grimstad days—is to compromise between two extremes. One extreme would be to break the cycle of repetitions, to strike out, through struggle and suffering, for genuine novelty, for a new contribution to the life of man. But this would be to enter the refining creative matrix of the universe and have one's ego shrunk to scale and eventually lost, becoming only a moment in the evolution of intelligence. The other direct route would be to face repetition undisguised, head on. To confront one's life as repetition is to confront oneself; to confront oneself in such terms is to confront despair; but to accept despair would be to affirm at least the potentiality of self-transcendence in other dimensions of existence. In either case, there would be a risk, a leap, but this time the real would be grounded in the real and the Button-molder sent packing. Peer's flirtation with pure research, however, is no more than another transitory bit of role-playing; and the first time he really knows despair is when the shooting star flashes down and out, and the mists shattered by his imaginary leap in the opening scene threaten to close in again. So, for the Gyntian personality, the cycle must hold; and the effective function of fantasy, in proceeding by roundabouts, we see, is to throw just enough of a veil over repetition to persuade the self that no really fundamental change or effort is necessary.

The great arc of the play's action, then—from Gudbrandsdal throughout the world and back again—though framed in the archetypal pattern of the hero's life, his adventure and return, is far from the fulfillment of a heroic destiny. In the three aspects of the play discussed above, comprising the hero's choice, his initiation and his quest, each is presented in terms of its inverse, its antithesis, the negative—or, as the Lean One makes clear, not even that, since, photographically speaking, Peer Gynt is an undeveloped plate on which nothing has really registered. In this antiromantic work that employs the full resources of the romantic theater, the nonheroic hero is the pilot model of the hollow man of our own time, rendered perplexed and anxious by problems of identity and direction.

"If the modern age has been rightly called the age of anxiety," Erich Fromm has written, "it is primarily because of . . . anxiety engendered by the lack of self." To the extent that we *are* all brothers in old Peer Gynt, Ibsen's image of the human condition takes its place as one of the invaluable reference points in mapping the present world and one of the major landmarks indicating the course of the past. Again, as Georg Groddeck remarks, there is so much to learn from this play, it is quite impossible to refer to everything.

Deficient as he is in a strong sense of self, Peer has a personality that picks up and reveals the pressures and conflicts of an age of transition the way iron filings strewn on paper bring out a magnet's lines of force. In his young manhood, Peer's life is outwardly restricted; he is the son of a *bondemand,* a peasant farmer, tied to his limited milieu of parish, village, and farm. The bent of his mind is feudal and romantically medieval; women are princesses, mountains are castles, trees are warriors cloaked in chain mail. He sees himself as a knight-at-arms, needing only an unapproachable lady to serve in the manner of the *fin aman.*

Then, with a masterfully bold stroke, Ibsen opens Act Four on his middle-aged protagonist's suavely presiding over the banquet years of the latter nineteenth century as an exemplar of the international, cosmopolitan world of finance capitalism. Peer has made his fortune, after the manner of the empire builders, in slaves and idols, the two logical products of reductive Gyntian opportunism, which turns even the essence of the human and the divine into commodities. (Appropriately, it is as an Americanized European that Peer engages in the slave trade, the shame of Europe and the guilt of America.)

The transition from an organic community based on land and blood ties, from which Peer Gynt is outlawed, to a collective based on abstract contractual relationships—the company of self-made men among whom he finds an insecure perch—is accompanied by the loosening, the blurring of traditional sanctions and prohibitions. The result is a state of inner disorientation and drift, the background of which can be traced through a number of literary antecedents. For, quite as much as the community defines for Oedipus what he has to do ("Now, Oedipus, Greatest in all men's eyes/here falling at your feet we all entreat you,/find us some strength for rescue"), so the Ghost in *Hamlet* lays his charge upon the prince ("If thou hast nature in thee, bear it not"). But, by the time of *Faust,* the bonds are clearly in dissolution; the hero has saved the community a long while back, and his present ties are rather with Mephistopheles, the destructive principle, conceived still in its traditional form. *Peer Gynt,* however, brings us up to date, as the hero wanders the whole world over, trying to discover what it is he ought to be or do. The community, the ancestors, even self-knowledge, are no longer sufficient guides. Life becomes a feat, or a series of feats, of subjective choice.

In this awareness, Kierkegaard had already modified the original Greek imperative accordingly. " 'Know thyself' cannot be the real goal of life," he wrote, "if it is not also the beginning. The ethical individual knows himself; but this knowledge is no mere contemplation. . . . It is a reflection about oneself, which is itself an action, and therefore I have purposely used the expression 'choose yourself' instead of 'know yourself.' " The transformation of the classic hero of reason and virtue, or the tragic departure therefrom, into the modern hero of the will, or the lack thereof, implies a new conception of tragedy, which Ibsen then strives to articulate. In the later plays, he is ceaselessly preoccupied with the question: To what extent *is* one free to choose oneself, and to what extent is self-knowledge, the uncovering of the obstinate past, a determinant in making that choice?

What is made clear in this earlier work is the fact that the hero is not free *not* to choose himself, not free to expand his personality in the romantic or Faustian pattern to include all knowledge, all experience, all phases of consciousness. It is part of its significance that *Peer Gynt* stands as a cenotaph for the Renaissance man.

At some time in the progressive nineteenth century with its immense and varied innovations in fact and theory, the Goethes, the Ben Franklins, the leisured men of parts, cease to be possible; and, with that abruptness that struck Henry Adams, the eighteenth-century man who was, at his best, still the Renaissance man, the microcosm of all learning, becomes the specialized twentieth-century man, locked in the pressure chamber of his career, seeking fulfillment in the utilitarian ethic. Peer experiments with that ethic briefly, after his manner, by envisioning himself as a canal builder, but the solution for the aged Faust is not for him. It is after this that he sees that, if he cannot be one thing, he must be all things; that he is, in reality, the sum of man, the whole of the past, the Emperor of all Human Life—but this last and greatest of his visions, which is essentially the Renaissance belief in the plenitude and perfectibility of the individual, is, by itself and in this advanced age, only one more waystage on the road to the Cairo asylum. Like his brother under the skin, Don Quixote, two and a half centuries before, Peer Gynt is a dreamer patching together the tatters of an outworn ideal, no longer of medievalism and *courtesie*—he has graduated from that —but of an aspiration that has its origins in Castiglione and Petrarch.

And what is Peer left with in the last analysis, under the tatters, under the patchwork coat of many colors? Only his life, his having lived, the fountain of his vitality. Every peeling of the onion—if one is looking for more in life—is a detour, a delusion; and yet at the same time, every peeling was himself, some part of himself that he could not deny. To give him due credit, we have to say of Peer that, in this one sense, he holds nothing back. There is no staid bourgeois façade, as in the later plays, in which chink after chink of the truth will open. And for this reason Groddeck is right when he speaks of him as sincere. For this is exactly what Peer Gynt is. This chronic liar whose life blows away like the desert wind, this clump of nothing who creeps back to the beginning and the end of everything in Solveig's lap, is amazingly sincere, amazingly significant. He was hardly far wrong about what he should do—what Ibsen did do with him—when, in the passage projecting the Renaissance ideal, he first thought of writing his life story down as a guide to others. But we, more fortunate, scarcely need his book when we have him alive in the theater. And with his flamboyance, his roguish variability, his innumerable masks and emotions, the theater is where he belongs, along with all the chiaroscuro of his motley world. Aase scolding on the hill, Peer spellbinding his mother into death, the near-blind Solveig speaking forgiveness at the end—in a theater of authentic, not counterfeit, greatness, they would prove unforgettable. The shifting illusions and realities of the stage are the counterpart and fit medium of the selfsame shifts within Peer's life, by which we are eventually brought up to that last and most impressive change of scene when, for him as perhaps for us, before the ultimate hour, a light breaks; and out of the strange mercy of the universe, the sun rises still one more time.

SELECTED BIBLIOGRAPHY

HENRIK IBSEN: THE MAJOR PLAYS

Love's Comedy   (1862)
Brand   (1866)
Peer Gynt   (1867)
Emperor and Galilean   (1873)
The Pillars of Society   (1877)
A Doll House   (1879)
Ghosts   (1881)
An Enemy of the People   (1882)
The Wild Duck   (1884)
Rosmersholm   (1886)
The Lady from the Sea   (1888)
Hedda Gabler   (1890)
The Master Builder   (1892)
Little Eyolf   (1894)
John Gabriel Borkman   (1896)
When We Dead Awaken   (1899)

SELECTED BIOGRAPHY AND CRITICISM

Bradbrook, M. C. *Ibsen, the Norwegian: A Revaluation.*
  London: Chatto & Windus, 1947; New York: The
  Macmillan Company, 1948.
Downs, Brian W. *Ibsen: The Intellectual Background.*
  London: Cambridge University Press, 1946; New York:
  The Macmillan Company, 1947.

————. *A Study of Six Plays by Ibsen*. London and New York: Cambridge University Press, 1950.

Groddeck, Georg. "Peer Gynt," in *Exploring the Unconscious*. New York: Funk & Wagnalls; London: Vision Press, Ltd., 1950.

Koht, Halvdan. *Life of Ibsen*. 2 vols. New York: W. W. Norton & Company, Inc., 1931.

Logeman, Henri. *A Commentary on Henrik Ibsen's Peer Gynt: Its Language, Literary Associations and Folklore*. The Hague: M. Nijhoff, 1917.

Lucas, F. L. *The Drama of Ibsen and Strindberg*. New York: The Macmillan Company; London: Cassell and Company, 1962.

Shaw, G. B. *The Quintessence of Ibsenism*. New York: Hill and Wang, 1957.

Valency, Maurice. *The Flower and the Castle, an Introduction to the Modern Drama: Ibsen and Strindberg*. New York: The Macmillan Company, 1963.

PEER GYNT

THE CHARACTERS

AASE, *a farmer's widow*
PEER GYNT, *her son*
TWO OLD WOMEN *with sacks of grain*
ASLAK, *a blacksmith*
WEDDING GUESTS. A CHIEF COOK. A FIDDLER, *etc.*
A NEWCOMER
HIS WIFE
SOLVEIG ⎱ *their children*
HELGA ⎰
THE FARMER AT HEGSTAD
INGRID, *his daughter*
MADS MOEN, *the bridegroom*
HIS PARENTS
THREE GIRLS *from a mountain farm*
A WOMAN IN GREEN
THE TROLL KING
A COURTIER TROLL. OTHERS SIMILAR. TROLL MAIDENS
    and TROLL CHILDREN. A PAIR OF WITCHES. GNOMES,
    GOBLINS, ELVES, *etc.*
A VOICE IN THE DARKNESS. BIRD CRIES
KARI, *a cottar's wife*
AN UGLY BRAT
MR. COTTON
M. BALLON ⎱ *traveling*
HERR VON EBERKOPF ⎰ *gentlemen*
HERR TRUMPETERSTRAALE
A THIEF *and a* FENCE

ANITRA, *daughter of a Bedouin chief*

ARABS. FEMALE SLAVES. DANCING GIRLS, *etc.*

THE STATUE OF MEMNON (*singing*). THE SPHINX AT GIZEH (*mute*)

PROF. BEGRIFFENFELDT, *Ph.D., director of the insane asylum at Cairo*

HUHU, *a language reformer from the Malabar coast*

A FELLAH *with a royal mummy*

HUSSEIN, *a Near Eastern government minister*

OTHER MADMEN, *along with their* KEEPERS

A NORWEGIAN SEA CAPTAIN *and his* CREW

A STRANGE PASSENGER

A PASTOR. MOURNERS

A SHERIFF

A BUTTON-MOLDER

A LEAN PERSON

The action opens in the early years of the nineteenth century and ends in the late 1860's. It takes place partly in Gudbrandsdal and the surrounding mountains, partly on the coast of Morocco, in the Sahara Desert, in a Cairo insane asylum, at sea, etc.

ACT ONE

❧

SCENE ONE

A wooded hillside near AASE's *farm. A stream runs brawling through, past an old mill set on its farther side. It is a hot summer day.* PEER GYNT, *a powerfully built boy of twenty, comes down the path.* AASE, *his mother, trails after him, angrily scolding.*

AASE
  Peer, you're lying!

PEER GYNT (*without stopping*)
                No, I'm not!

AASE
  Well, go on then—swear it's true!

PEER GYNT
  Swear? Why should I?

AASE
                Hah! Know what?
  You don't dare; they're lies right through!

31

PEER GYNT (*stops*)
　Every word's the gospel truth!

AASE (*confronts him*)
　No shame before your mother's wrath?
　First, it's the mountains, and you've skipped
　Out in my busiest month to go
　Tracking reindeer over the snow;
　Then come back with your coat all ripped—
　Not only no game, but you lose your gun!
　And if that's not enough, your big wide eyes
　Are dying to see me get taken in
　By the wickedest kind of hunter's lies.
　Now—where'd you come across this buck?

PEER GYNT
　West of Gendin.

AASE (*laughs derisively*)
　　　　　　　Oh, of course!

PEER GYNT
　I'm stalking down a wind that roars
　About me; hid up behind a grove
　Of alders, he's pawing in a pack
　Of snow for moss——

AASE (*as before*)
　　　　　　　　　Oh yes, of course!

PEER GYNT
　My breath stops short; I freeze and listen,
　Hear the scraping of his hoof,
　See a glint of antler horns.
　With that I'm flat between the stones,
　Worming up so's not to miss him.
　Then, screened by rocks, I feast my eyes on—
　Such a buck, so sleek and fat,
　You've never seen his equal yet!

AASE
　I'm sure of that!

PEER GYNT
　　　　　　　So bang! I shoot.

He hits the dirt, whump, like a mallet.
But in that instant as the brute
Lies still, I'm there astride his back,
Seize him by the left ear tight,
And poise to drive my knife in right
Below the jawbone for his gullet—
When hi! the scum lets out a shriek,
Scrambles bolt up on his feet
And, with this one head-backward flip,
Knocks knife and scabbard out of reach,
Clamps me neatly at the hip,
Rams his horns down on my legs
To pin me like a pair of tongs—
And then with dizzy leaps he springs
Along the brink of Gendin ridge! [1] *

AASE (*involuntarily*)
　Oh, my Jesus—!

PEER GYNT
　　　　　　　Have you seen
The way the cliffs of Gendin hang?
They run out nearly four miles long,
Lean as a scythe edge at the top.
Past glaciers, over granite slides
And gray herbs clinging to the slope,
You can look down either side
Straight into water, where in a slow
Black heavy sleep it lies one
Thousand yards, almost, below.
　He and I, on that blade of ground,
Cut a channel through the wind.
　I've never had me such a run!
Sometimes in the headlong pace
The air seemed full of flashing suns.
In the reeling gulfs of space
Eagles with brown backs would float
Midway between us and the water—
Then fall away behind, like motes.
　I could see ice floes crack and shatter

* References will be found on pp. 241ff.

On the shore, without a sound to hear.
Only the imps of swimming senses
Came singing, swirling, weaving dances
In rings around my eyes and ears.

AASE (*giddy*)
　Oh, God help me!

PEER GYNT
　　　　　　　Suddenly,
At a spot where the cliff drops violently,
This great cock ptarmigan explodes
Into wings, squawking terrified
From some nook where he'd thought to hide
Till the hoofs came on too loud.
　The buck goes spinning half around
And takes off with a tremendous bound,
Plunging both of us straight for the deep.

　　(AASE *sways and steadies herself against a tree.*
　　　　　PEER GYNT *continues.*)

Behind us, rock walls towering up,
Under us, blank nothingness—
And we two dropping, first through veils
Of mist, then through a flock of gulls
That wheel off, scattering their cries
To all the corners of the sky.
　Downward, endlessly, we go.
But in the depths something shows
Dim white, like reindeer's belly fleece.
Mother, it was *our* reflection
Shooting upward through the lake from
Silent darkness to the glassy calm
On top with the same breakneck
Speed as we were hurtling down.

AASE (*gasping for breath*)
　Peer! Dear Lord, what happened? Quick!

PEER GYNT
　My buck from above, the other
　From below lock horns together
　In one huge shower burst of foam.

We lie there, thrashing for a time.
Then at last, somehow, we make
It to the northern shore, the buck
Swimming, towing me in back of him—
So, here I am——

AASE

　　　　　But the reindeer?

PEER GYNT
Oh, I guess he's out there somewhere—

(*Snaps his fingers, turns on his heel, adding:*)

Finders keepers—you can have him!

AASE
And you didn't break your neck?
Or both your legs? What an escape!
You really didn't snap your spine?
Oh, great God—all thanks and praise
To Thee for delivering my son!
Your trousers got a little torn,
It's true; but that's of no concern
When you realize just how black
Things might have been after a leap—!

(*Stops abruptly, stares at him wide-eyed and open-mouthed, struggles for words until, at length, she bursts out.*)

Oh, you tricky little devil—
God in heaven, you can lie!
I remember all this drivel
Now; it happened to Gudbrand
Glesne, back when I was twenty.
This is his ride secondhand,
Not your own, you—!

PEER GYNT
　　　　　His *and* mine.
Things like that can happen twice.

AASE (*angrily*)
Yes, give a lie a new disguise,

Twist it, turn it out so fine
The bony carcass can't be seen
Spruced up in the fancy dress.
That's the only thing you've done—
Run wild in your imagination,
Trotted out those eagles' backs
And all your other filthy tricks,
Lied the sun and moon away,
And stirred up such a misery
Of fright that one forgets old
Things one heard once as a child.

PEER GYNT

If anyone else talked like that
To me, I'd cripple him for life!

AASE (*weeping*)

Oh, God, let me die; oh, let
Me sleep in the earth and rest!
Prayers and tears don't make him behave—
Now and forever, Peer—you're lost!

PEER GYNT

You pretty little mother, you,
Every word you say is true;
So just be happy, laugh——

AASE

                              Be still!
How can I be happy while
I have such a pig for a son?
Don't you think it's hard for me,
A helpless, struggling widow, to be
Always put to shame again?

          (*Once more weeping.*)

What have we got now from the days
When your grandfather's fortunes rose?
Those sacks of coin that Rasmus Gynt
Willed us—you know where they went?
Your father! Him, with his open hand,
And the money running through like sand,
Buying property right and left,

Driving his gilded carriages—
Where's it gone now, all the waste
Poured out for that winter feast
When the guests flung every glass
And bottle to the wall to smash?

PEER GYNT

Where are the snows of yesteryear? [2]

AASE

Don't talk back to your mother, Peer!
Look at the farm there! Nearly half
The windows plugged with rags and stuff.
Railings, fences, hedges down;
Cattle shifting to the wind and rain;
Fields and pastures gone to weeds;
And every month the sheriff takes——

PEER GYNT

That's enough of this old maid's
Talk! One's luck has losing streaks
Only to spring up good as new!

AASE

The ground is barren where it grew.
My Lord, what a country squire
You are! Swell-headed and cocksure,
Same as you were when the preacher
First came up from Copenhagen
And pried out your Christian name from
Your baby lips, then swore you had brains
To match any European prince,
So that your father, true to nature,
Went and gave him a horse and sleigh
For talking in such a kindly way.
Ah, but things looked rosy then!
Bishops, captains—how they all came
Flocking daily to drink and eat,
Stuffing themselves till they nearly split!
Who knows his friends in an easy time?
Nobody, not a soul, stopped in
The day "Jon Moneybags" took
To the road with a peddler's pack.

(*Drying her eyes with her apron.*)

Ah, Peer, you're big and strong;
You should be the mainstay now
That your mother's getting on—
Keep the farm in trim, and show
Some fight to save your nest egg.

(*With a new burst of tears.*)

Oh, God help me if I owe
Any thanks to you, you lazy slug!
Loafing in the chimney-corner
Home,[3] and poking up the fire,
Or out at dances where you scare
The local girls with your crazy manner—
You make me a common laughingstock;
And now, brawling with the lowest pack——

PEER GYNT (*moves away from her*)
Leave me alone.

AASE (*following him*)
     Go on, make
Believe you didn't lead that row
The other day at Lunde [4] when you
Boys all wound up swapping blows,
Mad as dogs. Oh, I suppose
It wasn't you that laid Aslak
The smith's arm up in a splint?
Or at least didn't you crack
One of his fingers out of joint?

PEER GYNT
Who fed you all that foolishness?

AASE (*hotly*)
Kari, downhill, heard the yelling!

PEER GYNT (*rubbing his elbow*)
Yes, but I made all the noise.

AASE
You?

PEER GYNT
       That's right—*I* got the mauling.

AASE
   What—?

PEER GYNT
          He can raise a bruise.

AASE
   Who can?

PEER GYNT
          He, Aslak, can. Who else?

AASE
   You—pah, you! I could spit!
   You mean a blubber-bellied sot,
   A walking sponge, a piece of tripe
   Like that could ever beat you up?

              (*Weeping again.*)

   Shame and scandal, how it fills
   My life—and now, worst of all, this
   Has to happen, this disgrace.
   Let him be brawny as an ox—
   Why should you be the one he licks?

PEER GYNT
   Win or lose, it doesn't matter—
   You boil me in the same hot water.

              (*Laughing.*)

   Ah, cheer up——

AASE
                 What! Were you lying
   Once again?

PEER GYNT
          Just this once.
   Dry your tears now; stop crying.

              (*Clenches his left hand.*)

Look—in these tongs, what chance
Did he have, bent double, glowing
Under the hammer of my right——

AASE

Oh, you fire-eater! You'll put
Me in the grave, the way you act.

PEER GYNT

Oh no, what you can expect
Is twenty thousand times finer
Than that! Dearest, ugly, little
Mother, be patient with it all:
This whole parish'll do you honor;
You just wait till I come out
With something—something really great!

AASE (*snorting*)
You!

PEER GYNT
Who knows what's in the cards?

AASE

If only someday you'd have sense
Enough to make an effort towards
Sewing the holes up in your pants.

PEER GYNT (*hotly*)
I'll be a king, an emperor!

AASE

An emperor? God help me, there
He's losing the little mind he had!

PEER GYNT
But I will! Just give me time!

AASE

Yes, time brings all things to him
Who waits, or so I've heard it said.

PEER GYNT
You'll see, Mother!

AASE

Hold your tongue!
The madhouse, that's where you belong—
    Still, you're not completely off—
Something is what you might have been
If you hadn't sunk yourself in
Lies and windy dreams and bluff.
The Hegstad girl was fond of you.
That plum was ripening to fall,
And would have, if you'd had the will——

PEER GYNT
Think so?

AASE

The old man hasn't got
The strength to tell his daughter "no."
He's strict with her, or tries to be,
But Ingrid always gets her way;
And where she goes, Old Stumble-shoe
Clumps after, angry as a beet.

(*Starts crying again.*)

Ah, my Peer, a girl with land,
Clear property, an heiress! Think—
If you'd only had the will,
You could have married into rank—
You, in your tatters, black as coal.

PEER GYNT (*briskly*)
Well, let's go courting someone's hand.

AASE
Where?

PEER GYNT
At Hegstad!

AASE

You poor child,
Your hopes are locked out in the cold.

PEER GYNT
What do you mean?

AASE
> Oh, it's too much!
> The moment's flown, and so's the luck——

PEER GYNT
> Why?

AASE (*sobbing*)
> While you went riding your buck
> Through the air over the western ridge,
> Mads Moen proved the plum was ripe.

PEER GYNT
> What—? That joke on women! Him!

AASE
> Yes, he's going to be the groom.

PEER GYNT
> Wait here till I harness up
> The horse and cart——

> (*Starts off.*)

AASE
> No use leaving.
> The wedding's set now for tomorrow.

PEER GYNT
> Ffft! I'll be there this evening!

AASE
> For shame! Don't you think my sorrow's
> Enough, without their ridicule?

PEER GYNT
> Don't worry; it'll all go well.

> (*Shouting and laughing at once.*)

> Hey, Mother! Let the cart stay here;
> There isn't time to get the mare.

> (*Lifts her in his arms.*)

AASE
> Put me down!

PEER GYNT
                No, like this you'll
Arrive in style on the wedding morn.

                (*Wades out in the stream.*)

AASE
   Help! Oh, God, be merciful!
   Peer! We'll drown——

PEER GYNT
                        I was born
   To die a nobler death——

AASE
                        That's true,
   Hanging's more in line for you!

                (*Pulls his hair.*)

   Oh, you monster!

PEER GYNT
                Now be calm;
   The footing here is slippery-smooth.

AASE
   Jackass!

PEER GYNT
              Yes, just use your mouth;
   Words do nobody any harm.
   There, you see, it's shelving up——

AASE
   Don't let me drop!

PEER GYNT
                Hi, giddap!
   Time to play at Peer and the buck——

                (*Cavorting about.*)

   I'm the reindeer, you be Peer!

AASE
   I don't know who I am, I swear!

PEER GYNT
  We're almost in the shallows, look—

                (*Wading ashore.*)

  So be nice, give the buck a kiss
  And thank him for the ride across——

AASE (*clouts him on the ear*)
  There's my thanks for the ride!

PEER GYNT
                      Ow!
  Your sense of gratitude is low.

AASE
  Let me go!

PEER GYNT
        To the wedding first.
  Be my spokesman. You're clever;
  Have a talk with the old crust;
  Tell him Mads is a real loafer——

AASE
  Let go!

PEER GYNT
        Then give him a chance to hear
  Something about *my* character.

AASE
  Oh yes, you can bet I will!
  You'll have a testimonial
  And your portrait painted front and back;
  I'll spill out every devil's trick
  I've seen you do, till his ears are limp——

PEER GYNT
  Oh?

AASE (*kicking furiously*)
        This tongue of mine will wag
  Until the old man sics his dogs
  On you, as if you were a tramp!

PEER GYNT
  Hm, then I'll have to go alone.

AASE
  Yes, but I'll be right behind you!

PEER GYNT
  Mother, you're not strong enough to——

AASE
  Strong enough? I feel so violent
  Inside that I could crumple stone!
  Hoo, I could make a meal of flint!
  Let go!

PEER GYNT
          All right, if you'll promise——

AASE
  Nothing! We're going, both of us.
  They have to find out what you are!

PEER GYNT
  No, you'd better stay right here.

AASE
  Never! I feel like some party life.

PEER GYNT
  I can't allow it.

AASE
          Give me a reason!

PEER GYNT
  I'll set you up on the millhouse roof.

          (*Lifts her up there.* AASE *screams.*)

AASE
  Get me down!

PEER GYNT
          Now will you listen——?

AASE
  Rubbish!

PEER GYNT
> I'm asking you, Mother dear——

AASE (*throws sod from the roof at him*)
> Get me down this instant, Peer!

PEER GYNT
> If I dared, you know I would.

> > (*Comes closer.*)

> Now, see if you can't stay quiet, glued
> To one spot. Try not to kick and flop
> About, and don't pull the shingles up—
> Or you might find out you've gone from bad
> To worse with a nasty fall.

AASE

> > > > You beast!

PEER GYNT
> Stop wiggling!

AASE

> > > Oh, for a wind to blast
> You like a changeling [5] off this earth!

PEER GYNT
> Mother, shame!

AASE

> > > Pah!

PEER GYNT

> > > Aren't I worth
> Your blessing in taking on this struggle?
> Can't you give it?

AASE

> > > I'll give a whipping
> To you for all your size, that's what!

PEER GYNT
> Then fare thee well, Mother, my sweet.
> Just be patient; I won't be long.

> (*Starts off, then turns and shakes his finger at her.*)

Remember now: you mustn't wiggle!

AASE

Peer! God help me, there he goes!
Reindeer rider! Liar! Hi!
Will you listen—? No; now he's
Running—! (*Shouts.*)
                    Help, I'm dizzy! Hurry!

(TWO OLD WOMEN, *with sacks on their backs, come
down the path toward the mill.*)

FIRST OLD WOMAN

Mercy, who's that screaming?

AASE

                    Me!

SECOND OLD WOMAN

Aase! You're rising in the world.

AASE

This much higher up is mild—
Wait till God lifts me up to glory!

FIRST OLD WOMAN

Happy journey!

AASE

                    Fetch a ladder;
Get me down! That devil Peer——

SECOND OLD WOMAN

Your son again?

AASE

                    You can consider
This as a sample of his behavior.

FIRST OLD WOMAN

We're witnesses.

AASE

                    If you'd just
Help me, I'd be at Hegstad fast——

SECOND OLD WOMAN
  Is he there?

FIRST OLD WOMAN
              You'll have vengeance now;
  The smith's gone off to the wedding too.

AASE (*wringing her hands*)
  Oh, God save me! The poor boy,
  They'll kill him, if they have their way!

FIRST OLD WOMAN
  It's time and again we've heard that talk;
  Take heart: if it's going to be, it will!

SECOND OLD WOMAN
  Her wits are scattering everywhere.

                    (*Calling up the hill.*)

  Eivind! Anders! Hey, come here!

A MAN'S VOICE
  What's the matter?

SECOND OLD WOMAN
                Peer Gynt's stuck
  His mother up on top of the mill!

SCENE TWO

*A small rise of ground covered with shrubs and
heather. Upslope and behind a fence runs the high
road.* PEER GYNT *comes along a footpath, hurries up
to the fence and stands gazing out over the land-
scape.*

PEER GYNT
  There it lies, Hegstad. I'll be there soon.

      (*Climbs half over the fence, then hesitates.*)

  Wonder if Ingrid's at home alone?

(*Shades his eyes and looks off.*)

No, the guests are swarming in like flies—
It might be better to just return.

(*Climbs down again.*)

They whisper behind your back, always
Sneering, and it sears you like a burn.

(*Goes a few steps from the fence and begins
aimlessly plucking leaves.*)

If I only had something strong to drink—
Or I could slip in without being seen—
Or just be unknown—— For numbing the pain
Of their laughter, nothing beats getting drunk.

(*Looks about him in a sudden fright, then hides
among some bushes. Several* WEDDING GUESTS, *with
presents, go by on the road toward the farm.*)

A MAN (*in conversation*)
With his father a drunkard—and that mother's a case.

A WOMAN
Yes, it's not hard to see why the boy's such a mess.

(*The* GUESTS *pass on. A moment later* PEER GYNT
emerges, blushing with shame, and stares after them.)

PEER GYNT (*softly*)
Were they speaking of me?

(*With a forced shrug.*)

　　　　　　　　　　Well, let them speak.
They can't kill the life in my veins with talk!

(*Throws himself down in the heather and lies on his
back awhile, hands under his head, gazing up into
the sky.*)

What an odd-shaped cloud! Like a horse almost,
Someone's riding him—he's saddled and reined—
And there's an old witch on a broom behind.

(*With a quiet little laugh.*)

It's Mother. She's scolding and yelling: "You beast!
Hi, wait for me, Peer!"

(*Slowly closing his eyes.*)

　　　　　　　　　　　She's frightened now—
Peer Gynt rides ahead, with an army in tow—
　　His harness is silver, his mount is gold-shod.
He wears gauntlets, a scabbard, a fine saber blade,
　　And a cape flowing long and silken-lined.
They're the salt of the earth, the men of his band;
　　Yet not one sits so bold in his saddle as Peer,
Or glitters like him in the sunlit air.
　　Below by the road people gather in groups,
Swinging their hats, and everyone gapes.
　　The women are curtsying. Who hasn't heard
Of the Emperor Peer Gynt and his thousand-man horde?
　　Pieces of silver and new copper coins
He scatters like sand till the pavement shines,
　　And every citizen's rich as a lord.
Then Peer makes the ocean his boulevard.
　　On a far-off shore stands Engelland's [6] prince,
And all Engelland's maidens wait in suspense.
　　And Engelland's nobles and Engelland's king,
As Peer canters up, rise from parleying.
　　The great king takes off his crown and speaks——

ASLAK THE SMITH (*to some others, passing on the road*)
　Well, look; it's Peer Gynt, the drunken swine—!

PEER GYNT (*half rising with a start*)
　My sovereign—?

ASLAK (*leaning over the fence and grinning*)
　　　　　　　　Get off your haunches, son!

PEER GYNT
　What the devil! Aslak! What do you want?

ASLAK (*to the others*)
　He's still hung up from his Lunde stint.

PEER GYNT (*springing up*)
　Get out of here.

ASLAK
>   Yes, I can do that.
But where have you been, lad? Out of sight
For six whole weeks. Trolls get you, what?

PEER GYNT
>   Aslak, I've done fantastic things!

ASLAK (*winks at the others*)
>   Give us the word, Peer!

PEER GYNT
>   Can't waste my lungs.

ASLAK (*after a pause*)
>   You going to Hegstad?

PEER GYNT
>   No.

ASLAK
>   They say
That girl there used to give you the eye.

PEER GYNT
>   You filthy crow—!

ASLAK (*drawing back a little*)
>   Easy now, Peer!
If Ingrid's dropped you, there's plenty more—
Think—Jon Gynt's son! Join the carouse;
There'll be tender lambs and bouncy widows——

PEER GYNT
>   Go to hell!

ASLAK
>   You'll find someone who'll have you.
Good day! I'll be giving the bride your love now.

(*They move on, laughing and whispering.* PEER
GYNT *stares after them briefly, then tosses his head
and turns half around.*)

PEER GYNT
Anyone Ingrid wants to marry

She's welcome to. Who gives a damn!

(*Inspecting himself.*)

Trousers torn. Ragged and grim—
I could use some new clothes in a hurry.

(*Stamps on the ground.*)

If I could just take a butcher's knife
And cut the mockery out of their chests!

(*Staring suddenly around.*)

What—! Who's that? Did somebody laugh?
Hm, I was sure—— Nothing but ghosts—
I'll go home to Mother.

(*Turns up the hill, stops again and stands, ears
cocked toward the farm.*)

The dancing's begun!

(*Gazing and listening, then moving downslope step
by step, his eyes kindling, his palms rubbing his
thighs*)

What a swarm of girls! Seven, eight to a man!
To hell and blazes! I can't go stale—
But Mother, perched on top of the mill—

(*His eyes are drawn back to Hegstad; he kicks up
his heels and laughs.*)

Ah, the halling! [7] How it floats and swirls
For Guttorm; how sweetly his fiddle's stroked—!
It sparkles and dips like a cataract.
And that flock, that shimmering flock of girls!
Oh, hell and blazes, I won't go stale!

(*Leaps the fence and heads down the road.*)

SCENE THREE

The grounds at Hegstad. Farthest to the rear, the farmhouse. A THRONG OF GUESTS. *Lively dancing on the grass. The* FIDDLER *is seated on a table. The* CHIEF COOK [8] *stands in the doorway.* KITCHEN MAIDS *go back and forth between the buildings.* OLD PEOPLE *sit here and there, conversing.*

A WOMAN (*joining a group seated on some logs*)
The bride? Oh yes, she's crying some,
For the usual reasons, mostly vague——

THE CHIEF COOK (*in another group*)
Now, folks, let's see you drain the keg.

A MAN
How—when you're filling it all the time?

A YOUTH (*to the* FIDDLER, *as he flies past with a girl by the hand*)
Hi, Guttorm, don't spare the bow!

THE GIRL
Scrape till you wake up every meadow!

OTHER GIRLS (*around a young man dancing*)
That's kicking!

A GIRL
                    He's got legs like steel!

THE YOUNG MAN (*as he dances*)
It's high to this ceiling [9] and wide to the wall!

(*The* BRIDEGROOM, *whimpering, comes up to his* FATHER, *who is talking to several others, and tugs at his sleeve.*)

BRIDEGROOM
Father, she won't; she's just too proud!

FATHER
  Won't what?

BRIDEGROOM
          She's locked herself away.

FATHER
  Well, it's up to you, then, to find the key.

BRIDEGROOM
  I don't know how.

FATHER
          You're a knucklehead!

          (*He turns back to the others. The* BRIDEGROOM
                    wanders off.)

A BOY (*rounding the house*)
  Hey, girls! The party's coming alive!
  Peer Gynt—!

ASLAK (*newly arrived on the scene*)
          Was he asked?

THE CHIEF COOK
                    Not by my leave.

          (*Goes into the house.*)

ASLAK (*to the girls*)
  If he starts talking to you, don't listen to him!

A GIRL (*to the others*)
  No. Pretend that we look right through him.

PEER GYNT (*hot and ardent, enters, stops in front of
          the group and claps his hands*)
  Which of you dancers can really move?

A GIRL (*as he approaches*)
  Not me.

ANOTHER
          Not me.

A THIRD
                    Nor me either.

PEER GYNT *(to a fourth)*
  All right, *you*—till some better ones gather.

THE GIRL *(turning aside)*
  Too busy.

PEER GYNT *(to a fifth)*
                  Then you!

THE GIRL *(as she leaves)*
                          I was just going home.

PEER GYNT
  So early? You must be out of your mind!

ASLAK *(after a moment, in a low voice)*
  See, Peer, she'll dance with the first man around.

PEER GYNT *(turns quickly to an elderly man)*
  Where are the unattached girls?

THE MAN
                          Find them.

(He walks away. PEER GYNT, *suddenly subdued, glances shyly and furtively at the group. They all look at him, but nobody speaks. He approaches other groups. Wherever he goes, there is silence; as he moves on, looks follow him and smiles.)*

PEER GYNT *(in an undertone)*
  Glances, hard thoughts and mocking smiles—
  They grate, like a saw blade under a file!

(He slinks along the fence. SOLVEIG, *leading little* HELGA *by the hand, comes into the yard with her parents.)*

A MAN *(to another, close by* PEER GYNT*)*
  Look, the new neighbors.

THE OTHER
                          From the west country, right?

FIRST MAN
  I think, from Hedal.[10]

THE OTHER
>Yes, that was it.

PEER GYNT (*steps in the newcomers' path and, pointing at* SOLVEIG, *asks her father*)
Can I dance with your daughter?

THE FATHER (*quietly*)
>You may; but first
We'll go in and pay our respects to the host.

(*They enter the house.*)

THE CHIEF COOK (*to* PEER GYNT, *offering him a drink*)
Since you're here, you'll want the bottle passed.

PEER GYNT (*staring fixedly after the newcomers*)
I'll be dancing, thanks. I have no thirst.

(*The* CHIEF COOK *moves away.* PEER GYNT *looks toward the house and laughs.*)

How fair! I've never seen a girl like this!
Looking down at her shoes and snow-white apron—!
And how she held onto her mother's dress,
And carried her prayer book wrapped in a napkin[11]—!
I must see her again.

(*Starts into the house, but is met by several young
men coming out.*)

A YOUTH
>You already the worse
For dancing?

PEER GYNT
>No.

THE YOUTH
>Then you're headed off course.
(*Takes his shoulder to turn him about.*)

PEER GYNT
Let me pass!

THE YOUTH
>Are you scared of the smith?

PEER GYNT
  Me scared?

THE YOUTH
          Ah, *that* memory still has teeth!

    (*The group laughs and goes on to the dancing.*)

SOLVEIG (*appears at the door*)
  Aren't you the boy that wanted to dance?

PEER GYNT
  Why, yes; didn't you know me at once?

                (*Taking her hand.*)

  Come on!

SOLVEIG
          Mother says, not too far.

PEER GYNT
  Mother says? Mother says! Were you born last year?

SOLVEIG
  You're making fun—!

PEER GYNT
                  But you're nearly a child.
  Are you grown?

SOLVEIG
          I'm just confirmed [12]—that old.

PEER GYNT
  Tell me your name, girl, and things'll go lighter.

SOLVEIG
  My name is Solveig. And who are you?

PEER GYNT
  Peer Gynt.

SOLVEIG (*draws back her hand*)
          Oh, my Lord!

PEER GYNT
                  What's wrong now?

SOLVEIG
　My garter's come loose; let me tie it tighter.

　　　　　　　　　(*Leaves him.*)

BRIDEGROOM (*pulling his mother's sleeve*)
　Mother, she won't—!

MOTHER

　　　　　　　She won't? Won't what?

BRIDEGROOM
　Just won't, Mother!

MOTHER

　　　　　　What?

BRIDEGROOM

　　　　　　　　　Unlock the door.

FATHER (*in quiet fury*)
　Uf! A stall—that's all you're good for.

MOTHER
　Now don't scold. Poor boy, he'll be all right.

　　　　　　　　(*They go off.*)

A YOUTH (*coming up with a crowd from the dancing*)
　Little brandy, Peer?

PEER GYNT

　　　　　　No.

THE YOUTH

　　　　　　　Ah, come on.

PEER GYNT (*looking somberly at him*)
　You have some?

THE YOUTH

　　　　　　Oh, it just might be.

　　　　(*Pulls out a pocket flask and drinks.*)

　Ai, that burns—! Well?

PEER GYNT

　　　　　　Let me see.

　　　　　　(*Drinks.*)

ANOTHER YOUTH
  Now you can have a taste of mine.

PEER GYNT
  No.

THE OTHER
      Ah, rubbish! Don't be a stupe.
  Drink up, Peer!

PEER GYNT
              Well, maybe a drop.

              (*Drinks again.*)

A GIRL (*in an undertone*)
  Come on, let's go.

PEER GYNT
              You afraid of me, puss?

A THIRD YOUTH
  Who isn't afraid of *you*?

A FOURTH
              We saw
  You in action at Lunde, you know.

PEER GYNT
  You should see me when I really cut loose!

FIRST YOUTH (*whispering*)
  Now he's started.

OTHERS (*thronging around in a circle*)
              Tell us! Say what
  You can do!

PEER GYNT
      Tomorrow——!

MORE VOICES
              No, now; tonight!

A GIRL
  Can you conjure, Peer?

PEER GYNT
>I can call up the devil.

A MAN
My grandmother, before I was born, did that!

PEER GYNT
Liar! What *I* do, no one can equal.
Once I conjured him inside a nut.
Through a wormhole, that is.

SEVERAL (*laughing*)
>Obviously!

PEER GYNT
He wept and swore and tried bribing me
With all kinds of things——

ONE OF THE CROWD
>But he had to remain?

PEER GYNT
Oh yes. I'd closed up the hole with a pin.
You should've heard him buzzing and booming——

A GIRL
Imagine!

PEER GYNT
>It was like a bumblebee humming.

THE GIRL
You still have him trapped in the nut?

PEER GYNT
>Oh, no,
The devil's made off on his own by now.
It's *his* fault the smith has it in for me.

A YOUTH
How come?

PEER GYNT
>I went to the smith and, "Say,"
I asked him, "could you crack this shell?"
"Sure"——and he laid it down on his anvil;

But that man's got a grip like a couple of hams
When he wields his sledge, so he just let fall——

VOICE FROM THE CROWD
Did he kill the devil?

PEER GYNT
                    He came down, wham!
But the devil was quicker and shot like a flame
Straight through the roof and split the walls.

SEVERAL VOICES
And the smith?

PEER GYNT
                    Just stood there with charred hands.
From that day on, we've never been friends.

(*General laughter.*)

MORE VOICES
That's a good one!

OTHER VOICES
                    It's nearly his best!

PEER GYNT
You think I'm inventing it?

A MAN
                    No, I agree
With you there; my grandfather told me most
Of this——

PEER GYNT
                    Liar! It happened to me!

THE MAN
Yes, everything has.

PEER GYNT (*tossing his head*)
                    Why, I can ride
Through the air like the wind going past!
The things I can do, the things—oh, God!

(*Another roar of laughter.*)

ONE OF THE CROWD
Peer, ride in the air a bit!

MANY VOICES
Yes, Peer, do——

PEER GYNT
Don't be so anxious begging me to.
I can ride like a hurricane over your lot,
And you'll fall, all of you, fall at my feet!

AN OLDER MAN
Now he's raving mad.

ANOTHER
What audacity!

A THIRD
Loudmouth!

A FOURTH
Liar!

PEER GYNT (*threatening them*)
You wait and see!

A MAN (*half drunk*)
You wait, and you'll get your coat dusted, hey!

OTHERS
Your back gone over! A fine black eye!

(*The crowd disperses, the older ones angry, the
younger ones laughing and jeering.*)

THE BRIDEGROOM (*close by* PEER)
Say, Peer, is it true you can ride in the air?

PEER GYNT (*brusquely*)
Anything, Mads! I'm a rare kind of man.

BRIDEGROOM
Then you have the invisible cloak, I'm sure.

PEER GYNT
  The hat, you mean? Yes, I have one.

  (*Turns from him.* SOLVEIG *comes across the yard,*
              leading HELGA *by the hand.*)

PEER GYNT (*goes toward them, his face lighting up*)
  Solveig! Oh, it's good to see you again!

  (*Seizing her by the wrist.*)

Now you're going to be swung and held!

SOLVEIG
  Let go of me!

PEER GYNT
              Why?

SOLVEIG
              You're much too wild.

PEER GYNT
  Wild like the reindeer when summer dawns.
  Come on, lass; don't be contrary!

SOLVEIG (*pulls her arm free*)
  I don't dare.

PEER GYNT
              Why?

SOLVEIG
              Because—you've been drinking.

  (*Moves away with* HELGA.)

PEER GYNT
  Oh, to feel my knife blade sinking
  Into the hearts of each and every
  One of them!

BRIDEGROOM (*nudging his elbow*)
              Help me get in to the bride?

PEER GYNT
The bride? Where is she?

BRIDEGROOM
            The storehouse.

PEER GYNT
                       So.

BRIDEGROOM
Oh, please, Peer, make an effort to!

PEER GYNT
No, you can do it without my aid.

(A thought strikes him. In a low, hard voice:)

Ingrid! The storehouse! *(Goes over to* SOLVEIG.*)*
          Now what do you say?

*(*SOLVEIG *turns to leave; he bars the path.)*

I look like a tramp, and it makes you ashamed.

SOLVEIG *(hastily)*
That's not true; I never dreamed—!

PEER GYNT
Yes! And I've gotten a little bit numbed.
But that was for spite, when you slighted me.
Come on!

SOLVEIG
         If I wished to, I still wouldn't dare.

PEER GYNT
Who are you scared of?

SOLVEIG
             Mostly my father.

PEER GYNT
Your father? I know; he's a living prayer!
The soul of piety,[13] eh? Well—answer!

SOLVEIG
  What should I answer?

PEER GYNT
                    Is he one of the saints?
  And you and your mother want everything nice?
  You going to answer?

SOLVEIG
                    Leave me in peace.

PEER GYNT
  No. (*In a low, bitter, intimidating voice.*)
      I can turn myself into a troll.
  I'll come to your bed at midnight, I will.
  If you hear something that hisses and grunts,
  Don't try to pretend it's only the cat.
  It's me, child! I'll drain off your blood in a cup;
  And your little sister—I'll eat her up;
  Because, you know—I'm a werewolf at night—
  I'll bite you all over the loins and back—

  (*Suddenly changes his tone and begs, as if in anguish.*)

  Dance with me, Solveig!

SOLVEIG (*looking darkly at him*)
                    What a nasty trick!

                    (*Goes into the house.*)

BRIDEGROOM (*wanders up again*)
  I'll give you an ox if you'll help me.

PEER GYNT
                    Come!

  (*They go behind the house. At the same time a
  crowd comes up from the dancing, most of them
  drunk. Noise and confusion.* SOLVEIG *and* HELGA,
  *their parents, and a number of older people come
  out the door.*)

THE CHIEF COOK (*to the* SMITH, *leading the crowd*)
  Calm down!

ASLAK (*pulling off his jacket*)
       We'll have a reckoning this time,
Till Peer Gynt or I get laid out flat.

SEVERAL VOICES
  Yes, let them fight!

OTHERS
       No, argue it out!

ASLAK
  We'll settle with fists; no more blather.

SOLVEIG'S FATHER
  Control yourself, man!

HELGA
       Will they hit him, Mother?

A YOUTH
  Let's tease him instead with all his lies!

ANOTHER
  Boot him out of here!

A THIRD
       Spit in his eyes!

A FOURTH (*to* ASLAK)
  You backing down?

ASLAK (*throwing his jacket away*)
       I'll murder the swill!

SOLVEIG'S MOTHER (*to* SOLVEIG)
  Now you see what they think of that fool.

AASE (*coming up with a stick in her hand*)
  Where's my son? He's getting it, fore and aft!
  Ah, the pleasure I'll have in walloping him!

ASLAK (*rolling up his shirt sleeves*)
  For his kind of carcass, a stick's too soft.

SEVERAL VOICES
  The smith's going to wring him!

OTHERS
>   Bung him!

ASLAK (*spitting on his hands and nodding at* AASE)
>   Hang him!

AASE
What! Hang my boy! Yes, try, if you dare—!
Me and my shadow, we'll leave you a scar.
Where is he? (*Calls across the yard.*)
>   Peer!

BRIDEGROOM (*running up*)
>   In the name of the faith!
Father, Mother, come—!

HIS FATHER
>   What next?

BRIDEGROOM
It's Peer Gynt——

AASE (*screams*)
>   Have they put him to death?

BRIDEGROOM
No, he's—! Look, up there on the rocks——

THE CROWD
With the bride!

AASE (*lets her staff sink*)
>   The beast!

ASLAK
>   It's a sheer drop;
But he climbs, God, like a goat on a crag!

BRIDEGROOM (*sobbing*)
Mother, how he carries her—just like a pig!

AASE (*shakes her fist at him*)
I hope you come plummeting—!

>   (*Shrieks in fright.*)

>   Hi, watch your step!

INGRID'S FATHER (*comes up, bareheaded, white with rage*)
  I'll have his life for stealing the bride!

AASE
  If I ever let you, God strike me dead!

ACT TWO

❦

SCENE ONE

A narrow path, high in the mountains. It is early morning. PEER GYNT *comes hurrying sullenly along the path.* INGRID, *partly dressed in bridal ornaments, tries to hold him back.*

PEER GYNT
  Just go away!

INGRID (*weeping*)
                After this!
  Where?

PEER GYNT
          Anywhere away from me.

INGRID (*wringing her hands*)
  Oh, you cheat!

PEER GYNT
              Don't make a fuss.
  We'd each better go off separately.

INGRID
  We're bound by sin—and sin again!

PEER GYNT
  Memories! The devil makes his home in
  Them; he lives in every woman—
  All but one—!

INGRID
                Who is that one?

PEER GYNT
  It isn't you.

INGRID
                What's her name?

PEER GYNT
  Go away! Back where you came from!
  To your father, quick!

INGRID
                        My dearest own—!

PEER GYNT
  Don't!

INGRID
          You can't possibly mean
  What you're saying.

PEER GYNT
                      I can and do.

INGRID
  Ruin me first—then cast me off!

PEER GYNT
  And what kind of future can you give?

INGRID
  Hegstad farm, and a lot more too.

PEER GYNT
  What do you wrap your prayer book in?
  Does your hair fall golden at your throat?

Do you gaze down into your apron?
Do you cling onto your mother's skirt?
Answer!

INGRID

No; but——?

PEER GYNT

And were you just
Now confirmed?

INGRID

No, but Peer——

PEER GYNT

Do I feel your shyness like a wound?
Can you refuse me what I ask for?

INGRID

Oh, God, I think he's lost his mind——!

PEER GYNT

Does the very sight of you bless the air?
Well!

INGRID

No, but——

PEER GYNT

Then what's all the rest?

(*Starts off.*)

INGRID (*blocking his way*)
Did you know it's a hanging crime
If you run off now?

PEER GYNT

I don't care.

INGRID

You could have property and honor
If you'd take me——

PEER GYNT

Can't afford them.

INGRID (*bursting into tears*)
    The way you coaxed——

PEER GYNT
                  You were willing!

INGRID
    I was desperate!

PEER GYNT
             And I was mad.

INGRID (*threatening*)
    You're not escaping till the price is paid!

PEER GYNT
    The highest price would seem like nothing.

INGRID
    Are you set on that?

PEER GYNT
              Like stone.

INGRID
    Good! We'll see who's going to win!

        (*Starts down the slope.*)

PEER GYNT (*silent a moment, then cries out:*)
    Memories! The devil makes his home in
    Them; he lives in every woman!

INGRID (*turns her head and calls up mockingly*)
    All but one.

PEER GYNT
            Yes, all but one.

        (*They go off separately.*)

SCENE TWO

*Soft marsh country near a mountain lake. A storm
is gathering.* AASE, *in despair, is peering in every di-*

rection and calling out. SOLVEIG *finds it hard to keep up with her.* SOLVEIG'S *parents and* HELGA *follow close behind.*

AASE (*flailing her arms and tearing her hair*)
Everything spites me with a vengeance—
Sky and water and these wicked mountains!
The sky pouring down fog to confuse him,
The water luring him in to seize him,
The mountains poising their rocks to fall—
And these people! All out for the kill!
Oh God, not that! I just can't lose him.
The lout! Why the devil has to tease him—?

(*Turning to* SOLVEIG.)

It's so unbelievable, it is,
That he who was always for dreams and lies,
He whose strength was all in his mouth,
Who'd never done work of any worth,
That he—! You want to both laugh and cry!
  Oh, we've had to stick close in misery.
Because, you know, my man—he drank,
Roamed the parish with a line of bluff,
Scattered and trampled our goods to dust—
While back at home my Peer and I sat.
All we could do was try and forget;
I'm no good at putting things to the test.
It's so painful staring fate in the eyes;
You'd much rather shake your troubles off
And just do anything not to think.
Some turn to brandy, others to lies,
And we—well, we took to fairy tales
Of princes and trolls and strange animals.
Stolen brides too. But who'd have thought
Those infernal stories would be in him yet.

(*Terrified again.*)

Hoo, what a scream! It's a troll or an ogre!
Peer! Peer! Up in the fog there—!

(*Runs to the top of a small rise and looks out over the lake.* SOLVEIG'S *parents come up.*)

Not a trace!

THE FATHER (*quietly*)
                 The worse for him.

AASE (*in tears*)
    Oh, my Peer, my poor lost lamb!

THE FATHER (*nodding gently*)
    Yes, he *is* lost.

AASE
                 That's not the same!
    He's so clever. There's nobody like him.

THE FATHER
    You foolish woman!

AASE
                      Yes, that's it,
    I'm a fool; but the boy's all right!

THE FATHER (*continues quietly, looking gently at her*)
    His heart's withered; his soul is lost.

AASE (*anguished*)
    Not true! The Lord isn't so unjust!

THE FATHER
    You think he could ever repent his sins?

AASE (*hotly*)
    No; but he and a buck have flown!

THE MOTHER
    Good grief, are you crazy?

THE FATHER
                      What was that!

AASE
    There's nothing he can take on too great.
    You'll find out, if he lives that long——

THE FATHER
    You'd be better off to see him hang.

AASE (*shrieks*)
Oh my Jesus!

THE FATHER
A length of rope
Might turn him toward our eternal hope.

AASE (*dazed*)
Oh, you'll talk me into a fainting spell!
Let's find him!

THE FATHER
To save his soul!

AASE
And skin!
If he's stuck in the marsh, let's bring him in;
And ring the church bells to scare off trolls.

THE FATHER
Hm—! Here's a cow path——

AASE
God repay
You for helping me!

THE FATHER
It's Christian duty.

AASE
Then they're heathens, all the others
Who wouldn't search, who couldn't bother—!

THE FATHER
They knew him too well.

AASE
He's above their likes!
(*Wringing her hands.*)
And to think—to think his life's at stake!

THE FATHER
Here's a man's footprints.

AASE
Better make sure!

THE FATHER
   We'll scatter downhill across the pasture.

                    (*He and his wife go ahead.*)

SOLVEIG (*to* AASE)
   Tell me some more.

AASE (*drying her eyes*)
                    Of my son?

SOLVEIG
                              Yes——
   Everything!

AASE (*smiles and throws back her head*)
              Everything—? You'll get tired of this.

SOLVEIG
   You'll be tired of talking long
   Before I'm through listening.

              S C E N E   T H R E E

*Low treeless knolls under a towering waste of moun-
tain; high peaks farther off. The shadows are length-
ening; it is late in the day.* PEER GYNT *comes
running full tilt and stops on the hillside.*

PEER GYNT
   The whole parish is hot on my track,
   Armed to the teeth with rifles and sticks!
   Old Hegstad's in front, you can hear him howl—
   The news is out, Peer Gynt's on the prowl!
   This is no row with a blacksmith here!
   This is life! I feel strong as a bear.

              (*Leaping in the air and lashing out.*)

   To crush, overthrow! Swim cataracts!
   Smash! Rip fir trees up by the roots!
   This is life! How it toughens and frees
   The soul! To hell with those sickly lies!

(THREE FARM GIRLS [14] *from a mountain hut come
running over the hill, shouting and singing.*)

FARM GIRLS
Trond of the Valfjeld! Kaare and Baard!
Trolls, come sleep with us, hold us hard!

PEER GYNT
Who're you shouting for?

FARM GIRLS
                    Trolls! For trolls!

FIRST GIRL
Trond, go easy!

SECOND GIRL
                Baard, be rough!

THIRD GIRL
The beds are all lying empty at home!

FIRST GIRL
Rough is easy.

SECOND GIRL
                And easy is rough!

THIRD GIRL
When there aren't any boys, a troll's good enough.

PEER GYNT
And where are your boys then?

ALL THREE (*roaring with laughter*)
                            They can't come!

FIRST GIRL
Mine called me near and dear as his shadow.
Now he's hitched to a middle-aged widow.

SECOND GIRL
Mine met a gypsy girl up north.
Now they're tramping the country earth.

THIRD GIRL
Mine put our bastard out of his pains.

Now his head sticks on a stake and grins.

ALL THREE
Trond of the Valfjeld! Kaare and Baard!
Trolls, come sleep with us, hold us hard!

PEER GYNT (*leaps in among them*)
I'm a three-headed troll [15] and a three-woman man!

THE GIRLS
You really perform?

PEER GYNT

Find out if I can!

FIRST GIRL
Up to the cabin!

SECOND GIRL

We've mead!

PEER GYNT

Let it flow!

THIRD GIRL
We won't have a bed lying empty now! [16]

SECOND GIRL (*kissing him*)
He sputters and glows like white-hot steel.

THIRD GIRL (*kissing him*)
With his baby eyes from a bottomless pool.

PEER GYNT (*dancing among them*)
Heart like a stone, blood like a goat,
Eyes full of laughter, tears in the throat!

THE GIRLS (*thumbing their noses at the mountaintops,
    shouting and singing*)
Trond of the Valfjeld! Kaare and Baard!
Did you sleep with us once? Did you hold us hard?

(*They dance away over the heights with
    PEER GYNT in their midst.*)

SCENE FOUR

In the Ronde Mountains.[17] *Sunset. Snow-capped
mountains gleaming on all sides.*

PEER GYNT (*enters, wild and distraught*)
Castle on castle soaring!
See, what a glittering gate!
Stay! Will you stay! It's veering
Farther and farther about!
The cock on the weathervane's lifting
His golden wings into flight.
He fades in a blue mist, drifting;
The mountains freeze in for the night.
    What are those trees there, rooted
In crevasses of the rock?
They're warriors, heron-footed!
Now they're passing into the dark.
    The air, like a rainbow streaming,
Cuts into my eyes and soul.
What far-off bells are chiming?
What's pressing down on my skull?
My head swells bigger and bigger;
It's clamped in an iron band—!
I can't for the life of me figure
How that got wrapped around!

(*Sinks down.*)

A race along Gendin's ridges.
Dreams and damnable lies!
Straight over the sheerest ledges
With the bride—then a drunken daze;
Hunted by hawks and falcons,
Menaced by trolls and gnomes,
Wenching with crazy women—
Lies and damnable dreams!

(*Gazing up for a long time.*)

Way up there, two brown eagles.
Southward, a flight of geese.
And here I wallow and straggle
Through mud and filth to the knees!

(*Springing up.*)

I'll join them! Wash myself clean in
A bath of the flurrying winds!
Fly to the heights, then dip down in
The waters and rise up christened!
I'll skim the mountain cabins,
Glide till my spirits dance,
Soar out over rolling oceans,
And high over Engelland's prince!
Look up from below, young maidens;
My flight can't ease you at all;
Your waiting is only a burden—
Well, I might drop down for a while.
    That's funny. Those two eagles—?
They've vanished, devil knows where—
    Wait! There's the peak of a gable,
And now the eaves coming clear,
Sprung up from the ruins—yes,
And look, the gate's open wide!
Why, I remember that house:
Grandfather's farm in its pride!
The rags are gone from the windows;
The fences are straight and tall.
Light blazes from every pane now;
They're feasting in the great hall.
    I can hear a chinking of metal;
It's the bishop's knife on his glass—
Now the captain's flinging his bottle,
And the mirror shivers to smash.
Let's squander! This is tremendous!
Hush, Mother; who says we can't!
The rich Jon Gynt's behind us—
Three cheers for the house of Gynt!
What's that? Pandemonium
Breaking out at the feast—?
The captain calls me to join him;

The bishop makes me a toast.
Go in, Peer, in where your fate is
Sung out in prophecy:
Peer Gynt, thou art born of greatness,
And greatness is coming to thee!

> (*Leaps forward, but bangs his nose
> against a rock and falls senseless.*)

SCENE FIVE

*A hillside with great sighing shade trees. Stars
twinkle through the leaves; birds sing in the tree-
tops. A* WOMAN IN GREEN [18] *walks on the slope.*
PEER GYNT *follows her, making all sorts of amorous
gestures.*

WOMAN IN GREEN (*stops and turns*)
Is that true?

PEER GYNT (*drawing his finger across his throat* [19])
                    True as my name is Peer,
And true as you're a beautiful woman!
Will you have me? You'll see the way I care;
You won't ever have to weave or spin—
Just eat; and the meals will be immense.
I'll never pull your hair, not once——

WOMAN IN GREEN
Nor beat me, either?

PEER GYNT
                    Am I the type?
We kings' sons don't beat our women up.

WOMAN IN GREEN
You're a king's son?

PEER GYNT
                    Yes.

WOMAN IN GREEN
                    I'm the Dovre King's daughter.

PEER GYNT
    You are? Well, that's a coincidence.

WOMAN IN GREEN
    Deep in the Ronde his castle stands.

PEER GYNT
    My mother's is bigger, if it's any matter.

WOMAN IN GREEN
    You know my father? His name's King Brose.

PEER GYNT
    You know my mother? Her name's Queen Aase.

WOMAN IN GREEN
    When my father's mad, the mountains flinch.

PEER GYNT
    When my mother scolds, there's an avalanche.

WOMAN IN GREEN
    My father can kick to the highest beams.

PEER GYNT
    My mother rides through the swiftest streams.

WOMAN IN GREEN
    Have you no other clothes than those fish nets there?

PEER GYNT
    Ah, you should see my Sunday gear!

WOMAN IN GREEN
    Weekdays, I'm always in gold and silks.

PEER GYNT
    It looks more to me like celery stalks.

WOMAN IN GREEN
    Yes, but there's one thing to understand
    About Ronde customs: here you'll find
    Everything has to be seen two ways.
    You could easily think, if you went on
    To my father's court, that his royal house
    Was nothing more than a bleak moraine.

PEER GYNT
  Well, isn't it just the same with us?
  Our gold would look to you like dross,
  And every glittering pane might seem
  Like clouts of stockings, rags and grime.

WOMAN IN GREEN
  Black seems white, and vile looks fair.

PEER GYNT
  Great seems small, and foul looks pure.

WOMAN IN GREEN (*embracing him*)
  Oh Peer, I can see, we're like one and the same!

PEER GYNT
  Like a leg for a trouser; like hair for a comb.

WOMAN IN GREEN (*calls off across the hill*)
  My steed, my steed! My bridal steed!

(*An enormous pig comes running in, with a rope
end for a bridle and an old sack for a saddle.* PEER
GYNT *swings up onto its back and sets the* WOMAN
IN GREEN *in front of him.*)

PEER GYNT
  Giddap! Straight for the Ronde gate, ride!
  Hi, come on, boy! Up we go!

WOMAN IN GREEN (*caressingly*)
  And I was just feeling so sad and blue—
  How life provides, if you give it a chance!

PEER GYNT (*whips the pig to a trot*)
  Great men show in the style of their mounts.

S C E N E   S I X

*The Royal Hall of the King of the Dovre Moun-
tains.* [20] *A great assembly of* TROLL COURTIERS,
GOBLINS *and* GNOMES. *The* TROLL KING *sits on his
throne, sceptered and crowned. His* CHILDREN *and*

CLOSE RELATIVES *are grouped around him.* PEER
GYNT *stands before him. Wild uproar in the hall.*

TROLL COURTIERS
Kill him! A Christian's dared to lure
The Dovre King's most beautiful girl!

A TROLL CHILD
May I slash his finger?

ANOTHER
               May I tear his hair?

A TROLL MAIDEN
Please, let me bite him in the rear!

TROLL WITCH (*with a ladle*)
Shouldn't we boil him down for gruel?

ANOTHER WITCH (*with a carving knife*)
Turn him on a spit, or have him for stew?

THE TROLL KING
Cool your blood!

      (*Beckons his counselors to him.*)

             It's no time to crow.
We've been slipping downhill these later years—
Who knows if things'll go better or worse,
So let's not discourage a new recruit.
Besides, the boy looks perfectly fit,
And he's well set up, if I see him clear.
It's true, he hasn't a head to spare,
But my daughter's only a one-headed troll.
Three-headed trolls have gone out of style;
You scarcely see two-headers any more,
And the ones you do see are pretty poor.

         (*To* PEER GYNT.)

So—it's my daughter you want to have?

PEER GYNT
Yes, and your realm for the dowry too.

TROLL KING
    You can have half while I'm still alive,
    And the other half right after I go.

PEER GYNT
    That's fair enough.

TROLL KING
                    Just a minute, boy—
    There are some promises you have to give.
    Break only one, and the contract's clay,
    And you'll never get out of here alive.
    First, you must promise never to care
    For the world beyond our own frontier;
    Renounce day, deeds, the things of light.

PEER GYNT
    If I can be king, there's nothing to that.

TROLL KING
    Next—I'll put your wits to the test——

            (*Draws himself up on his throne.*)

THE OLDEST COURTIER TROLL (*to* PEER GYNT)
    Let's see if your wisdom tooth can
    Crack the shell of our king's request!

TROLL KING
    What's the difference between a troll and a man?

PEER GYNT
    No difference, so far as I can see.
    Big trolls roast you, and little trolls claw—
    Same as with us, when our feelings show.

TROLL KING
    Yes, there and in other points, we agree.
    But morning is morning and night is night,
    And there *is* a difference down at the root.
    I'll tell you what it is. Outside,
    Among men, under the shining sky,
    They say: "Man, to yourself be true!"
    While here, under our mountain roof,
    We say: "Troll, to yourself be—enough!" [21]

THE COURTIER TROLL (*to* PEER GYNT)
Can you fathom that?

PEER GYNT

Through a dark cloud.

TROLL KING
My boy, "enough"—that severing term—
Must blaze forth from your coat of arms.

PEER GYNT (*scratching behind his ear*)
Well, but——

TROLL KING

It *must,* if you want to rule here!

PEER GYNT
Well, all right, I guess that's fair——

TROLL KING
Next, you must sing the praises of
Our simple, domestic way of life.[22]

    (*He gestures; two trolls with pig's heads
and white nightcaps bring food and drink.*[23])

Our cows give cake and our bulls give mead;
Don't ask how it tastes, sour or sweet;
The main thing that you must never forget
Is—it's made here at home, and not abroad.

PEER GYNT (*pushing the things away*)
To hell with all your homemade brews!
I'll never get used to this country's ways.

TROLL KING
The bowl belongs with the drink; it's gold.
Who owns this bowl, my daughter will hold.

PEER GYNT (*musing*)
It's written: Thou shalt purge thy nature—
In time the drink may seem less sour.
So, bottoms up! (*Drinks.*)

TROLL KING

Ah, shrewdly put.
You spit?

PEER GYNT
> One trusts to the force of habit.

TROLL KING
> Now, throw off your Christian dress.
> Everything's mountain-made with us;
> From the valleys we get nothing else
> But the silk bows that adorn our tails.[24]

PEER GYNT (*angrily*)
> I have no tail!

TROLL KING
> We'll get you one.
> Steward, my Sunday best! Tie it on.

PEER GYNT
> Lay off! You think I've lost my mind?

TROLL KING
> You can't court my daughter with a smooth behind.

PEER GYNT
> Turn man to a beast!

TROLL KING
> My son, you're wrong;
> I just want you fit for dallying.
> You'll get a flame-yellow bow to wear,
> And that rates the highest honors here.

PEER GYNT (*thoughtfully*)
> Well, they say that man is only a mote,
> So custom and fashion should guide us a bit.
> Tie away!

TROLL KING
> You're most cooperative.

COURTIER TROLL
> Let's see how well you can wag your tail!

PEER GYNT
> Ha, there's more you want of me still?
> Would you also like my Christian faith?

TROLL KING

No, you can hold that under your breath.
Faith is free; we impose no tax;
A troll is known by the way he looks.
Once we're the same in manners and clothes,
You're free to believe in the things we loathe.

PEER GYNT

You know, despite the conditions you make,
You're more sensible than I thought you'd be.

TROLL KING

Trolls aren't as bad, son, as people say;
It's one other point where we're unalike—
Well, that ends the party's serious side;
Now we'll enjoy what our senses bring—
Musician! Strike the Dovre harp strings!
Dancer! Let the floor echo your tread!

(*Music and dance.*)

COURTIER TROLL

How do you like it?

PEER GYNT

                    Hm——

TROLL KING

                              Speak out.

What do you see?

PEER GYNT

                    A horrible sight.
A bell cow strumming a catgut lyre,
And a sow in stockings dancing to her.

COURTIERS

Eat him!

TROLL KING

              He sees us in human terms,
Remember!

TROLL MAIDENS

              Tear out his eyes and ears!

WOMAN IN GREEN (*sobbing*)
    Hu-hu! The things we have to endure
    Whenever my sister and I perform!

PEER GYNT
    Oh no, was it you? My little taunts,
    You know, were only offered in fun.

WOMAN IN GREEN
    Do you swear to that?

PEER GYNT
                The music and dance,
    So help me—seemed uncommonly fine.

TROLL KING
    It's strange about this human nature,
    Just how remarkably deep it goes.
    If it gets gashed in some battle with us,
    It heals right up and wears its scar.
    Now my son-in-law's mild as any man;
    He willingly dropped the garb of a Christian,
    Willingly drank the bowl of mead,
    Willingly let his tail be tied—
    In fact, was so willing in all we made him
    Do that I really thought the old Adam
    Had at last been safely kicked out of doors;
    But, look, in a wink he's back in force.
    Ah yes, my son, you need the cure
    For this unnatural human nature.

PEER GYNT
    What do you mean?

TROLL KING
                I'll crease your left eye
    A little, till you see things slant—
    But all you see will make you content.
    Then I'll cut out the right windowpane——

PEER GYNT
    Are you drunk?

TROLL KING (*puts some sharp implements on the table*)
            See, these are glazier's tools.

You'll be blinkered like an angry bull.
Then you'll discover your bride's a queen,
And your sight will never again confuse
Her beauty with pigs or musical cows.

PEER GYNT
You're raving mad!

THE OLDEST COURTIER
                      You heard what he said;
It's he who's wise, and you that's mad.

TROLL KING
Think of the torments, the miseries
You'll save yourself in afterdays.
Vision, don't forget, is the source
Of tears, and the body's bitter light.

PEER GYNT
That's true; and there's the Bible verse:
"If thine eye offend thee, pluck it out."
Wait! But tell me, when would it mend
Back to human sight?

TROLL KING
                      Never, my friend.

PEER GYNT
Hm! Well, then I'll say thanks, but no.

TROLL KING
Where are you heading?

PEER GYNT
                      It's time to go.

TROLL KING
Hold on! Here it's easy to enter in,
But the gate's not made to swing out again.

PEER GYNT
You're not going to keep me here forcibly?

TROLL KING
Now listen, be reasonable, Prince Peer!
You're gifted for trollhood. Doesn't he bear

Himself already quite trollishly?
And you want the job—?

PEER GYNT

Of course I do.
For a bride, and a well-run empire to boot,
There are losses I can accommodate.
Everything has its limits, though.
I've taken a tail, that I'll admit;
But what's been tied, my hands can unknot.
I've shed my trousers; they were old and thin,
But I'm sure I can button them on again.
And I'm sure as well that I can slough off
All signs of your Dovre way of life.
I'll gladly swear that a cow is a woman;
An oath one can always whistle away—
But *this*—to know you can never be free,
Never die decently as a human,
To run as a hill troll till kingdom come—
It's this—the fact that you can't go home
The way the book says, *this* you're intent on;
But it's what I'll never put my consent in.

TROLL KING

Now, bless my sins, I'm getting cross;
And I'll have no more of this foolishness.
You whey-faced runt! I won't be used!
You've gone for my daughter a bit too fast——

PEER GYNT

You lie in your teeth!

TROLL KING

You must marry her.

PEER GYNT

You dare to accuse me—?

TROLL KING

What? Can you swear
She hasn't gone flickering through your lust?

PEER GYNT (*snorting*)

Is that all? Who's going to make *that* stick?

TROLL KING

　You human beings are all alike.
　You honor the spirit with your lips
　And settle for what your hands can keep.
　So you think that desire doesn't matter?
　You'll soon have visible proof, just wait——

PEER GYNT

　You're not catching me with your liar's bait!

TROLL KING

　Peer, by the year's end, you'll be a father.

PEER GYNT

　Open up; let me out.

TROLL KING

　　　　　　　　　　You'll get the brat
　Wrapped in a goatskin.

PEER GYNT (*mopping sweat from his brow*)
　　　　　　　　　　Oh, to wake up!

TROLL KING

　Should he go to your palace?

PEER GYNT

　　　　　　　　　　　　To anyone's doorstep!

TROLL KING

　Splendid, Prince Peer; you can arrange it.
　But one thing is certain: what's done is done,
　And your child will burgeon up like a weed;
　These mongrels ripen remarkably soon.

PEER GYNT

　Now don't be so stubborn-minded, Dad.
　Be sensible, girl. Let's compromise.
　I'm neither a prince nor rich, God knows—
　And no matter how you measure or weigh me
　You're not going to gain much profit by me.

　　　(*The* WOMAN IN GREEN *faints and is carried
　　　　out by the* TROLL MAIDENS.)

TROLL KING (*gives him a look of utter contempt*)
  Dash him to bits on the rocks, children!

TROLL CHILDREN
  Can we play owl and eagle then?
  The wolf game! Gray mouse and glow-eyed cat!

TROLL KING
  Yes, quickly. I'm vexed and sleepy. Good night!

(*He leaves.*)

PEER GYNT (*hunted by* TROLL CHILDREN)
  Let go, you devils!

(*Starts to squirm up the chimney.*)

TROLL CHILDREN
          Come, goblins! Gnomes!
  Bite his back!

PEER GYNT
        Ow!

(*Tries the cellar trapdoor.*)

TROLL CHILDREN
        Plug all the seams!

COURTIER TROLL
  What sport for the young!

PEER GYNT (*struggling with a tiny troll, who has bitten
    deep in his ear*)
          Let go, you toad!

COURTIER TROLL (*raps his knuckles*)
  Careful, you bully; that's royal blood.

PEER GYNT
  A rathole—! (*Runs toward it.*)

TROLL CHILDREN
        Gnomes! Turn him elsewheres!

PEER GYNT
  The old man was foul, but the children are worse!

TROLL CHILDREN
  Flay him!

PEER GYNT
                    Oh, to be small as a mouse!

                         (*Runs aimlessly.*)

TROLL CHILDREN (*swarming about him*)
  Close in! Surround him!

PEER GYNT (*in tears*)
                              The size of a louse!

                         (*He falls.*)

TROLL CHILDREN
  Now, at his eyes!

PEER GYNT (*buried in a heap of trolls*)
                         Help, Mother, I'll die!

                    (*Church bells ring far off.*)

TROLL CHILDREN
  Bells in the mountains! Blackfrock's cows! [25]

     (*The trolls flee in a turmoil of howls and shrieks.
     The hall collapses; everything vanishes.*)

                    S C E N E   S E V E N

  Pitch blackness. PEER GYNT *can be heard striking
  and flailing about with the branch of a tree.*

PEER GYNT
  Speak out! Who are you?

A VOICE IN THE DARKNESS
                         Myself.

PEER GYNT
                              Move aside!

THE VOICE
  Go roundabout, Peer! The ridge is wide.

PEER GYNT (*starts to go through at another point, but
    is stopped by something*)
　　Who are *you*?

THE VOICE
　　　　　　Myself. Can you say the same?

PEER GYNT
　　I can say what I please; and my sword rams home!
　　Look out! Ahh! Now he feels his wounds!
　　King Saul killed hundreds; Peer Gynt, thousands!

　　　　　(*Hewing and slashing.*)

　　Who are you?

THE VOICE
　　　　　　Myself.

PEER GYNT
　　　　　　　That fool answer
　　You can keep; it makes nothing clear.
　　What are you?

THE VOICE
　　　　　　The great Boyg.[26]

PEER GYNT
　　　　　　　　I see!
　　The riddle was black, and now it's gray.
　　Out of the way, Boyg!

THE VOICE
　　　　　　Go roundabout, Peer!

PEER GYNT
　　Straight through! (*Striking out.*) He's down!

　　　　　(*Tries to go on, but again is stopped.*)

　　　　　What? Still more?

THE VOICE
　　The Boyg, Peer Gynt! The one only one.
　　The Boyg that's unhurt, and the Boyg that's in pain.
　　The Boyg that's dead, and the Boyg that's alive.

PEER GYNT (*flinging the branch away*)
  The sword's bewitched, but fists are enough.

(*Hammers his way ahead.*)

THE VOICE
  Yes, trust to your fists, your body's hope.
  Ho-ho, Peer Gynt, you'll get to the top.

PEER GYNT (*returning*)
  Forward and back, it's just as far.
  Out or in, it's a narrow door.
  He's *there*! And *there*! And beyond the bend!
  As soon as I'm out, he rings me around—
  Your name? Let me see you! Say what you are!

THE VOICE
  The Boyg.

PEER GYNT (*groping about*)
          Not dead, nor alive. Slime; gray air,
  Not even a form. It's like trading jabs
  With a den of snarling, half-awake bear cubs.

(*Shrieks.*)

  Stand up to me!

THE VOICE
          The Boyg's not insane.

PEER GYNT
  Strike!

THE VOICE
          The Boyg doesn't strike.

PEER GYNT
                    Fight! Come on!

THE VOICE
  The Boyg doesn't fight—and doesn't lose.

PEER GYNT
  For a gnome on my back, raking his spurs!
  Or only so much as a year-old troll!

Something to fight with. But there's nothing at all—
Now he's snoring! Boyg!

THE VOICE

What?

PEER GYNT

Use force!

THE VOICE
The great Boyg conquers in quietness.

PEER GYNT (*bites himself in the hands and arms*)
Gashing teeth and claws in the flesh!
I've got to feel my own blood drop.

(*A sound like the wingbeats of great
birds* [27] *is heard.*)

BIRD CRIES
Boyg, is he coming?

THE VOICE

Yes, step by step.

BIRD CRIES
Sisters far off, fly down in a rush!

PEER GYNT
If you want to save me, girl, do it quick!
Don't gaze at your apron, chaste and coy—
The prayer book! Fling it straight in his eye!

BIRD CRIES
He wanders!

THE VOICE

We have him.

BIRD CRIES

Sisters, attack!

PEER GYNT
If the price of life is this agony,
Even one hour's too much to pay.

(*Sinks down.*)

THE BIRDS
Boyg, he's fallen! Take him! End him!

     (*Church bells and hymns in the distance.*)

THE BOYG (*dwindles to nothing, his voice a gasp*)
He was too strong. There were women behind him.

SCENE EIGHT

Sunrise. On the slope by AASE'S *mountain hut. The door is bolted; everything is deserted and still.* PEER GYNT *lies asleep along one wall. He wakes, looks about with a dull, heavy stare, then spits.*

PEER GYNT
Oh, what I'd give for a pickled herring!

     (*Spits again, and at the same moment notices*
      HELGA *approaching with a food basket.*)

Well, what brings you up here, child? Exploring?

HELGA
It's Solveig——

PEER GYNT (*leaps up*)
           Where is she?

HELGA
                    Back of your hut.

SOLVEIG (*hidden*)
Come any closer, and I'm going to run!

PEER GYNT (*stops*)
Afraid you'll wind up in the arms of a man?

SOLVEIG
Shame on you!

PEER GYNT
          Know where I was last night?
The Troll King's daughter chased me like a hornet.

SOLVEIG
   It's a good thing, then, that we rang the bells.

PEER GYNT
   Don't worry, Peer Gynt's not the one to fall—
   What'd you say?

HELGA (*bursting into tears*)
                Oh, she's running! Wait!
   Wait for me! (*Hurries after.*)

PEER GYNT (*seizing her arm*)
             Look, what's here in my pocket!
   A silver button. You can have it too—
   Only, speak well of me!

HELGA
             Please, let me go!

PEER GYNT
   It's yours.

HELGA
        Please—there's food in the basket!

PEER GYNT
   If you don't, God help you——

HELGA
              You upset me!

PEER GYNT (*gently, releasing her*)
   No, I mean—ask her not to forget me!

          (HELGA *runs off.*)

ACT THREE

SCENE ONE

*Deep in a pine forest. Gray autumn weather, with
snow falling.* PEER GYNT *stands in his shirt sleeves,
felling timber. He is hewing away at a great fir with
crooked branches.*

PEER GYNT
Ah, you're tough, you old partisan—
But all the same, you're going to fall.

   (*Hewing away again.*)

I see you're wearing a coat of mail;
Strong as it is, I'll stave it in.
Go on; shake your crooked arms;
Your anger puts you out of form;
But still you're going to bow to me—!

   (*Breaks off abruptly.*)

Lies! It's just a battered tree.
Lies! It's no armor maker's work;

Only a fir with peeling bark.
It's weary labor, chopping wood,
But to chop *and* dream is crazy mad.
I'm through with it—this life of mist
That weaves the living moment past.
You're an outlaw, Peer! A hunted beast.

(*Chopping hard for a time.*)

An outlaw, yes. No mother about
To bring you food when it's time to eat.
If you're hungry, boy, you're on your own;
Take it raw from woods or stream;
Split your kindling, build your fire,
Putter and mend and make secure.
If you want warm clothing, kill a buck;
If your house needs shoring, break the rock;
If you're short of timber, fell the logs
And haul them in on aching legs.

(*The ax sinks; he gazes off.*)

It can have splendor. A tower and vane
On the ridgepole, soaring high and clean.
And then I'll carve, for the end of the gable,
A mermaid, fish-shaped down from the navel.
The vane and the locks will be of brass—
And panes of glass I'll try to get.
Strangers passing will wonder what
It is that shines on this distant rise.

(*Laughs angrily.*)

Infernal lies! I'm wandering back.
You're an outlaw, Peer!

(*Chopping fiercely.*)

                    A plain bark roof
Against the weather is quite enough.

(*Looks up at the tree.*)

There, he's swaying. Now, just a kick—
And he'll topple and cut a shuddering swath
Through all this tangled undergrowth!

*(Starts to trim off branches; suddenly
he listens, motionless, ax in midair.)*

Someone's after me—! Is that your kind,
Old Hegstad—that you have to sneak around?

(Crouches behind the tree and peeps out.)

A boy! And alone. He looks afraid.
He's staring about. What is that, hid
By his jacket? A sickle. His eyes keep scanning—
Now he's spreading his hand on the fence rail.
Now what? Why does he stand there, leaning—?
Ugh, his finger, it's off! He's cut
The whole finger off! He bleeds like a bull—
He's running away with his fist in a clout.

(Rises)

The devil! An irreplaceable finger—
Lost! And not to anyone's anger.
Ah, now I know—! That's the price
For getting out of his army service.
That's it. They want to send him to war;
And the boy, of course, doesn't want to go—
But to cut off—? For all time, never to—
Yes, think it; wish it; *will* it so—
But to *do* it! No, that's not for Peer.

(Shakes his head quietly, then returns to work.)

SCENE TWO

A room in AASE'S *house. Everything in disorder,
boxes standing open, clothing strewn about, a cat
lying on the bed.* AASE *and* KARI *are hard at work,
packing and straightening up.*

AASE *(running to one side of the room)*
   Kari, listen!

KARI
            What now?

AASE (*back to the other side*)
> Tell me—!
> Where's—? Where did I—? You know, where's the—?
> What do I want? My mind's a turmoil!
> Where's the key to the chest?

KARI
> In the keyhole.

AASE
> What's that rumbling?

KARI
> The last cartload
> Going over to Hegstad.

AASE (*weeping*)
> I'd be glad
> To be going, too, in a long black box.
> Ah, but life brings its share of heartbreaks!
> Merciful God! The house stripped bare!
> What old Hegstad left, the sheriff took—
> Down to the very clothes on my back.
> The shame of a justice so unfair!

> (*Sitting on the edge of the bed.*)

> The farm and the land, lost to our name.
> Hegstad hurt us; but the law was a crime—
> No one to help; no mercy given;
> Peer far away; no counsel even—

KARI
> But the house is yours till the day you die.

AASE
> Yes, I and the cat can take charity!

KARI
> God help you, Aase; you've paid for your son.

AASE
> Peer? Now that's an odd opinion!
> Ingrid got home safe, finally.
> They ought to lay the blame on the devil—

He's the power in all that's evil;
The prince of hell betrayed my boy!

KARI

Maybe I'd better send for the pastor?
You might have worsened without your knowing.

AASE

The pastor? I guess it would be best for—

(*Starting up.*)

God no, I can't! What am I saying?
His mother must help him; it's the least I owe—
To be there when the others turn away.
They left him this coat. I'll patch it up.
Ah, the fur rug's something I'd like to keep!
Where are the stockings?

KARI

There, in that muddle.

AASE (*rummaging around*)
What's this—? Look, it's the casting ladle
From the old days! With this he used to play
Button-molder—melt and pour and ply
The metal. At a party once, he came in
And asked his father for a lump of tin.
"Not tin," says Jon, "but coin of the mint—
Silver, because you're the son of Jon Gynt."
God save him, he was a little wild
From drink, and couldn't tell tin from gold.
There, the stockings. And full of holes!
They could stand darning.

KARI

They really could.

AASE

When that's been done, I'll go to bed.
I feel so poor, so sick and depressed—

(*Joyfully.*)

Two wool shirts, Kari—these they missed!

KARI
  So they did.

AASE
                 It's something at least.
  One of them's yours; we can settle with
  That—or—no, we can take them both.
  The one he's got is wearing thin.

KARI
  But, Mother Aase, stealing is sin!

AASE
  Oh well, but you know the pastor brings
  Forgiveness for this, and all our wrongs.

                  S C E N E   T H R E E

*Outside a newly built hut in the forest. Reindeer
antlers over the door. The snow lies deep. It is dusk.*
PEER GYNT *stands in front of the door, fixing a
large wooden bar in place.*

PEER GYNT
  There must be a bolt, one that can fasten
  This door against trolls, and women and men.
  There must be a bolt, one that can lock
  The goblins out, all the merciless pack.
     They come with the dark; they hammer and hit:
  "Open up, Peer Gynt, we're as quick as thought!
     We're under the bed, in the ash of the fire;
  We stream down the chimney like dragons. Ah, Peer—
     What made you think that nails and slats
  Could shut out the merciless goblin thoughts?"

  (SOLVEIG *comes across the snowfield on skis; she has
     a shawl over her head and a bundle in her hand.*)

SOLVEIG
  God lighten your work. Don't turn me away.
  I've come to your call; now let me stay.

PEER GYNT
 Solveig! It can't be—! Oh, but it is!
 And you're not afraid to come so close!

SOLVEIG
 Your call reached out in my sister's voice;
 It came on the wind and in silences.
 In your mother's words I felt it flame;
 And it echoed out of my waking dreams.
 The heavy nights, the empty days
 Kept calling me, telling me, "Go where he goes."
 My joy was gone, my life cut short;
 I couldn't laugh or cry from my heart.
 I couldn't be sure what your feelings were;
 I only knew I had to come here.

PEER GYNT
 But your father?

SOLVEIG
     On this whole wide earth
 I've no one for father or mother both.
 I've left them forever.

PEER GYNT
     Solveig, my own—
 You did this for me?

SOLVEIG
     Yes, for you alone;
 You must be all to me—lover and friend.

    (*In tears.*)

 The worst was leaving my sister behind—
 No, leaving my father, *that* was the worst;
 But still worse, to leave her whose breast
 Had nourished me; oh, God, no, the real
 Pain and sorrow was leaving them all!

PEER GYNT
 You know the judgment read last spring?
 I'm stripped of my farm, of everything.

SOLVEIG
> You think I cast off the ones I love
> Just for some property you might have?

PEER GYNT
> You've heard the sentence? Outside this wood
> I'm fair game for all, with a price on my head.

SOLVEIG
> I asked my way here with each turn of the climb;
> They said, "Why go there?" I said, "It's my home."

PEER GYNT
> Then away, away with these nails and slats!
> Who needs bars against merciless thoughts?
> If you can dare live in my hunter's house,
> This ground will become a holy place.
> Solveig! Let me look at you! Not too near!
> Only to look at you! Oh, how pure and fair!
> Let me lift you! But you're slender and light!
> I could carry you forever and feel no weight!
> I won't ever soil you. These arms, Solveig,
> Will hold your lovely, warm body from me!
> Who would have thought I could win your love?
> Oh, the nights, the days, and the longing I've—
> Look, you can see how I've built my hut;
> But it's coming down; it's mean and squat——

SOLVEIG
> Mean or great—it suits my mind.
> It's so easy to breathe against this wind.
> Down there it was stifling, closed like a trap;
> That was partly what drove me up.
> But here, where the firs cut the sky like gems,
> What stillness and song! Here I'm at home.

PEER GYNT
> Are you sure of that? For as long as you live?

SOLVEIG
> The path I've chosen doesn't swerve.

PEER GYNT
> Then you're mine! Go in! Let me see you indoors.

Please! I'll get some roots for a fire.
In that bright warmth, that cozy glow,
You can be safe; you won't freeze now.

(*He opens the door, and* SOLVEIG *enters. He stands
silent a moment, then laughs with joy and leaps
in the air.*)

My princess! At last, she's found and won!
Now my palace will rise on a true foundation!

(*He picks up his ax and starts off; at the same
moment, an* OLD WOMAN *in a tattered green gown
comes out of the wood; an* UGLY BRAT *with a
flagon in his hand limps after, holding onto her
skirt.*)

THE WOMAN
Good evening, Peer Lightfoot!

PEER GYNT
                              Hello, who's there?

THE WOMAN
Old friends, Peer Gynt! Our place isn't far.
We're neighbors.

PEER GYNT
                    Oh? That's more than I knew.

THE WOMAN
As your hut built up, mine built itself too.

PEER GYNT
I'm in a rush——

THE WOMAN
                    You always were;
But I'll track you down and get you for sure.

PEER GYNT
You've made a mistake, woman!

THE WOMAN
                              Only once;
That time you promised me into a trance.

PEER GYNT
I promised——? What fool kind of nonsense is that?

THE WOMAN
You've forgotten you drank with my father one night?
You've forgotten——?

PEER GYNT
                    Yes; what I've never known.
What *is* this? When did we meet last? When?

THE WOMAN
We met last—the day we met first.

(*To the* BRAT.)

Give Daddy a drink; he suffers from thirst.

PEER GYNT
Daddy? You're drunk! Do you call him——?

THE WOMAN
You know it's bacon when you see the rind!
Where are your eyes? Don't you see, he's lame
In his leg as you're lame in your mind.

PEER GYNT
You mean to imply——?

THE WOMAN
                    You mean to protest——?

PEER GYNT
That gangling brute——!

THE WOMAN
                    He grew up fast.

PEER GYNT
You troll snout, leave me out of your fix——

THE WOMAN
Now, Peer, you're bellowing like an ox!

(*Crying.*)

How can I help it if I'm less beautiful
Than when you lured me on that heathery hill?

Last fall in my labor, the fiend held my back,
So it's no surprise I've a twisted look.
If you want to see me fair as before,
Turn that creature away from your door,
Tear her out of your mind and sight—
Do that, my love, and I'll lose my snout!

PEER GYNT
Get away, you witch!

THE WOMAN
                    Just see if I do!

PEER GYNT
I'll split your skull!

THE WOMAN
                    Try! Let's see you!
Ho-ho, Peer Gynt, I can take your blows!
I'll keep coming back till the end of your days.
I'll squint through the door and spy on you both;
And if you sit with your girl by the fire—
And start to caress—and put off your clothes—
I'll slip in between and take my share.
She and I, we'll have you by turns.
So marry her, Peer, while your pleasure burns!

PEER GYNT
You nightmare of hell!

THE WOMAN
                    Oh, I nearly forgot!
My light-footed love, you can raise the brat.
There, pet, run to your daddy?

THE BRAT (*spits at him*)
                    Pfft!
I'll take the ax to you—wait, just wait!

THE WOMAN (*kisses the* BRAT)
Oh, but there's a head on that boy!
You'll be your father now any day.

PEER GYNT (*stamping*)
I could wish you as far—!

THE WOMAN

                    As now we're near?

PEER GYNT (*clenching his fists*)
    And all this—!

THE WOMAN

                Merely for thoughts and desires!
    It's hard on you, Peer!

PEER GYNT

                    Worse for another—!
    Solveig, my treasure, my true delight!

THE WOMAN

    "How the innocent suffer," said the devil to his mother,
    When she whacked him because his father got tight!

    (*She plods off into the forest, followed by the* BRAT,
        who hurls the flagon back toward PEER.)

PEER GYNT (*after a long silence*)
    "Roundabout," said the Boyg. I have no choice—
    My palace is ruined, shivered to bits!
    There's a wall around her. We came so close—
    Now the world's turned foul; my happiness rots.
    Roundabout, lad! There's just no way
    Straight through to her—no, not for you.
    Straight through? Hm, there ought to be—still—
    There's a text on repentance, I seem to recall.
    But what? What is it? I've forgotten the words,
    Don't have the book; and there's no one to guide
    My footsteps here in this trackless wood.
        Repentance? It might wear on for years.
    Till I fought my way through. That's no life.
    To shatter what's holy and pure, what I love,
    Just to bind it together in cracks and scars?
    That works for a fiddle, but not for a bell.
    If you want a field green, keep it free of your heel.
        But that was a lie, that with the troll snout!
    Now the corruption's all out of sight—
    Yes, out of sight, but not out of mind.
    Thoughts pursue me like whimpering hounds.
    Ingrid! And the three who danced on that crest!

Will they appear too? Cry out, with their storms
Of laughter, like her to be hotly embraced?
Roundabout, boy. Were my arms as long
As the fir tree's root or the river's tongue,
I think I'd be holding her still too near
To set her down again holy and pure.
    Let me work it around, this way or that,
So I manage neither to gain nor lose.
Just push it away and try to forget——

(*Goes several steps toward the hut and stops.*)

    Go in after this? So foul and coarse?
Go in, with all this odor of troll?
Speak, but be silent; confess, but conceal?

(*Throws the ax away.*)

It's a holy-day evening. For me to approach
The way I am now, would be sacrilege.

SOLVEIG (*in the doorway*)
Are you coming?

PEER GYNT

                    Roundabout!

SOLVEIG

                                What?

PEER GYNT

                                You must wait.
It's dark here, and I've something heavy to get.

SOLVEIG
Wait, I'll help you. We'll share to the full.

PEER GYNT
No, stay where you are! I'll carry it all.

SOLVEIG
Please, not too far!

PEER GYNT

                    Be patient, my sweet;
Far or near—you must wait.

SOLVEIG
> Yes, I'll wait!

(PEER GYNT *goes down the path to the forest.* SOLVEIG *remains standing in the open half-door.*)

SCENE FOUR

AASE'S *hut. Evening. A log fire throws its light on the walls. The cat is on a chair at the foot of the bed, where* AASE *lies, pulling restlessly at the sheets.*

AASE
> Lord God, why doesn't he come?
> The hours drag endlessly by.
> I've no way of sending to him,
> And terribly much to say.
> There isn't a moment to lose!
> So soon! How little we know!
> If I'd thought it would end like this,
> I'd never have scolded him so!

PEER GYNT (*comes in*)
> Good evening.

AASE
> God bless you, dear!
> Oh, my boy! So you did come then!
> But what are you doing down here?
> Your life's at stake near town.

PEER GYNT
> My life? It's not worth a hang.
> I just had to see your face.

AASE
> This proves that Kari was wrong;
> And I can go out in peace.

PEER GYNT
> Go out? What are you saying?
> Where do you want to go?

AASE

Ah, Peer, there's no denying—
It's plain that my time is due.

PEER GYNT (*writhing and pacing the floor*)

I've run from one heavy weight;
I thought at least *here* I'd be free—!
Are you cold in your hands and feet?

AASE

Yes, Peer; but it soon goes away—
When my eyes begin to glaze,
You must carefully close each lid.
And see to my coffin, please;
Take care it's the finest wood—
Oh no, I forgot——

PEER GYNT

                    Be still!
There's plenty of time for that.

AASE

Yes, true. (*Looks restlessly about.*)
                You can see how little
They left. That's them, all right.

PEER GYNT (*wincing*)

Again! (*Sharply.*)
                I know I'm to blame.
But why must you hammer it in?

AASE

You? No, the demon rum;
That's what struck us down!
You know you'd been drinking, Peer;
And so your wits were dulled;
And then you'd been riding reindeer—
No wonder you acted wild!

PEER GYNT

All right, let that story drop.
Enough of that whole display.
Whatever is heavy we'll keep—
Till later—some other day.

(*Sits on the edge of the bed.*)

Mother, let's talk, you and I—
But only of this and that.
Things that are twisted and wry,
That hurt—we can forget—
Ah, look! It's the old cat;
Is he really still alive?

AASE

He screeches so in the night;
You know what that's warning of!

PEER GYNT (*turning away*)
What's the news of the parish?

AASE (*smiling*)
They say there's a girl who's bent
On the uplands with every wish——

PEER GYNT (*quickly*)
Mads Moen, is he content?

AASE

They say that she's stopped her ears
To her father's and mother's pleas.
If you saw her a moment, Peer—
You might give her good advice——

PEER GYNT

And Aslak, he's getting ahead?

AASE

Don't speak of that filthy smith.
Let me tell you the girl, instead;
Her name's on the tip of my breath——

PEER GYNT

No, let's talk now, you and I—
But only of this and that.
Things that are twisted and wry,
That hurt—we can forget.
You're thirsty? Do you want a drink?
Have you room? That bed's like a toy.
Let me see—but, yes, I think

It's the one I had as a boy!
Remember the evenings you sat
By my bedside when I was young
And tucked me under the coverlet
And sang me ballad and song?

AASE

Of course! And when your father
Was out, then we played sleighs.
The spread was a lap robe of fur,
And the floor was a sheet of ice.

PEER GYNT

Yes, but all else above—
You remember, Mother, too—?
The dashing horses we drove——

AASE

Yes, don't you think I know—?
Our cat, and that other one—
Kari's; we had her on loan.

PEER GYNT

To the Castle East of the Sun
And the Castle West of the Moon,
To Soria-Moria Castle [28]
The high and the low roads wound.
You had a whip with a tassel—
It was just a stick we'd found.

AASE

I drove like a real cavalier——

PEER GYNT

Yes, you reined the horses loose;
And you'd turn as the hoofs struck fire,
Always afraid I might freeze.
Bless you, you dear old relic,
You did have a loving soul—!
Why did you moan?

AASE

               My back.
It's these hard boards I feel.

PEER GYNT
  Here take a better position.
  There now; more comfortable?

AASE (*restlessly*)
  No, I want to move on!

PEER GYNT

                    Move on?

AASE
  Just to keep moving—that's all.

PEER GYNT
  Pah! Let me tuck in the coverlet.
  Like so. If the night seems long,
  We'll shorten it. There; I'll sit
  And sing you ballad and song.

AASE
  No, my Bible! I'll read the Apostle.
  My thoughts are weighing me down.

PEER GYNT
  In Soria-Moria Castle
  There's a feast for the king and queen.
  Lie back on the silken cushion;
  We'll drive there over the snow.

AASE
  But—have I an invitation?

PEER GYNT
  Why, of course! Both of us do.

  (*He throws a cord round the chair where the cat
    lies, picks up a stick, and sits on the end of the bed.*)

  Gee-up! Get along, Blackie!
  Mother, you're not going to freeze?
  Ho, but the ride goes quickly
  When Grane [29] sets the pace!

AASE
  Dear heart, what is it, that ringing—?

PEER GYNT
    The silver sleighbells you heard!

AASE
    But those hollow echoes thronging?

PEER GYNT
    We're galloping over a fjord.

AASE
    I'm frightened! What is that roaring
    Like some great, hungry mouth?

PEER GYNT
    Only the night wind tearing
    Through the branches on the heath.

AASE
    Far off there, something glimmers.
    What makes that wavering blaze?

PEER GYNT
    The castle's doors and windows.
    Can you hear them dancing?

AASE
                              Yes.

PEER GYNT
    Saint Peter stands at the main door;
    He's motioning you to come in.

AASE
    He greets me?

PEER GYNT
                    Yes, with honor,
    And pours out the sweetest wine.

AASE
    Wine! Are there cakes as well, Peer?

PEER GYNT
    In droves! The finest sort.
    And the pastor's wife, his helper,
    Makes you coffee and dessert.

AASE
  My Lord, will she and I meet?

PEER GYNT
  As easy and free as you like.

AASE
  You mean it? Peer, what a banquet
  They're giving for my poor sake!

PEER GYNT (*cracking his whip*)
  Hup! Get along there, Blackie!

AASE
  You're sure, dear, this is the way?

PEER GYNT (*cracks it again*)
  Yes, the broad road.

AASE
             I feel shaky
  And weak from this racketing sleigh.

PEER GYNT
  I can see the castle so close;
  The race is just about run.

AASE
  I'll lie back and rest my eyes
  And trust it to you, my son.

PEER GYNT
  Press on, Grane, my pacer!
  The courtyard's filled to the brim;
  They swarm to the portals and stare.
  Peer Gynt and his mother have come!
  Saint Peter, what did you say?
  My mother may not come in?
  You could look till the seas run dry
  To find a worthier woman!
  Of myself, I won't say a word;
  I can turn at the castle gate
  If you take me, I'll be flattered;
  If not, I won't be put out.
  I've made up more lies already

Than the devil learning to preach,
And called my mother "Old Biddy"
For the way she'd cackle and scratch.
But you give her love and honor,
Make her at home in your truth.
They don't come up any finer
From the parishes of our faith.
Ho-ho, there's God the Father!
Saint Peter, you're in for it now!

(*In a deep voice.*)

"An end to this fuss and bother—
Mother Aase can come in free!"

(*Laughs aloud and turns to* AASE.)

Isn't *that* how I said it would break?
Now they're singing a different tune!

(*Anxiously.*)

Mother! That faraway look!
It's as if your wits had flown!

(*Goes to the head of the bed.*)

Don't stare! Your eyes are like china.
Mother, speak! It's me, your son!

(*Cautiously feels her forehead and hands, then throws the cord on the chair and says quietly.*)

So that's it. You can rest now, Grane.
The long haul is really done.

(*Closes her eyes and bends over her.*)

Here's thanks for all of your days,
For the blows and the kisses I had—
But give back some little praise—

(*Presses his cheek to her mouth.*)

There—that was thanks for the ride.

KARI (*entering*)
What? Peer! So then we're beyond

Our heaviest sorrow and dread!
Dear Lord, but she's sleeping sound.
Or is she—?

PEER GYNT

Shh. She's dead.

(KARI *weeps over the body;* PEER GYNT *walks slowly about the room, finally coming to a stop by the bed.*)

PEER GYNT
See that she's buried worthily.
It's time that I quit this soil.

KARI
Are you going far?

PEER GYNT

To the sea.

KARI
So far?

PEER GYNT

Yes; and farther still.

(*He goes out.*)

ACT FOUR

SCENE ONE

The southwest coast of Morocco. Under an awning in a palm grove, a table, on rush matting, set for dinner. Farther back, hammocks slung from the trees. A steam yacht, flying Norwegian and American flags, lies offshore. On the beach, a jolly boat. It is near sundown. PEER GYNT, *a handsome, middle-aged man in an elegant traveling suit, gold pince-nez dangling at his chest, presides at the head of the table.* MR. COTTON [30] *and* MONSIEUR BALLON, *along with* HERR VON EBERKOPF [31] *and* HERR TRUMPETERSTRAALE,[32] *are finishing dinner.*

PEER GYNT
Gentlemen, drink! If man is made
For pleasure, let his pleasure thrive.
As somebody wrote: the past is dead,
What's done is done—— Now what'll you have?

TRUMPETERSTRAALE
As a host, brother Gynt, you're enormous!

PEER GYNT

> I share the honor with my purse,
> My steward and my cook——

COTTON

> 　　　　　　　Very well,
> A toast to the four. Here's to them all!

BALLON

> Monsieur, you have *un goût, un ton*
> Nowadays so rarely found
> In gentlemen living *en garçon*—
> A certain—how shall I say—?

EBERKOPF

> 　　　　　　　A shade
> Of introspection, more than a drop
> Of world-historical-fellowship,[33]
> A vision piercing through the clouds,
> The most unprejudiced of minds
> Stamped by the higher criticism,
> An *Ur-natur,* a microcosm,
> All in one living opus blent.
> Is so, monsieur, that's what you meant?

BALLON

> But of course—though it lacks a tinge
> Of beauty it might have had in French.

EBERKOPF

> *Ei was!* That language, much too stiff—
> But if we wish to seek the ground
> Of phenomena——

PEER GYNT

> 　　　　　That's been found.
> It's why I've forgone married life.
> Gentlemen, indeed, things are
> Very clear. What should a man be?
> I say *himself* and nothing more.
> All for *himself* and *his!* I say
> Why, like a camel, should he carry
> Somebody else's load of worry?

EBERKOPF

   But this In-and-for-yourselfness
   Must have cost a struggle, I'm sure——

PEER GYNT

   Oh yes, back in the early years;
   But my honor was never at a loss.
   Once I nearly put my leg
   Into a trap that Cupid laid.
   I was a gay and salty dog,
   And the lady that I coveted—
   She was born of royal blood——

BALLON

   Born of royal—?

PEER GYNT (*carelessly*)
              The real old stock,
   You know the sort——

TRUMPETERSTRAALE (*slaps the table*)
               Those titled brats!

PEER GYNT (*with a shrug*)
   Thin-blooded snobs, the kind that take
   Their pride in a family record book
   Free of the least plebeian blot.

COTTON

   You mean your courtship hit a snag?

BALLON

   Her parents thwarted the alliance?

PEER GYNT

   Quite the reverse.

BALLON

           Ah!

PEER GYNT (*forbearingly*)
              Well, you see,
   There was a growing reason why
   The marriage better be held at once.
   But, to be frank, the whole business

Right from the start made me recoil.
In certain ways, I'm fastidious,
And I like an independent role.
And so, when her father came around
Insinuating his demand
That I shed my name and occupation
To dance in the puppet show of fashion,
Along with other requests as well,
Irksome, if not impossible—
Why then, gracefully, out I bowed,
Gave him his ultimatum back—
And renounced my budding bride.

(*Drumming on the table with a pious air.*)

Yes, there's a Fate behind our luck!
We mortals can rely on it—
And gather comfort in the thought.

BALLON
　　But—was the matter really closed?

PEER GYNT
　　Oh no; that I discovered next.
　　Some high-strung relatives got mixed
　　Up in it and violently aroused.
　　The worst was the family's younger set.
　　With seven of them I fought a duel.
　　It's a time I never will forget,
　　Although I weathered the ordeal.
　　It cost me blood; but that same blood
　　Confirmed my birthright to be great,
　　And boldly pointed, as I said,
　　To the wise design of Fate.

EBERKOPF
　　These life principles you offer
　　Rank you as a philosopher.
　　For, while the common-sense observer
　　Views the world in scattered scenes
　　And gropes his stumbling way forever,
　　Your mind orders and combines;
　　All things measure to your norm.

You point up isolated rules
And truths till they radiate like beams
Of light from Philosophy's pure soul.
And you've had no formal education?

PEER GYNT

I am—I'm happy to repeat—
A man exclusively self-taught.
My studies have had no discipline;
But fed by thought and speculation
And random reading, my mind has grown.
I started rather late in life;
And then, as you know, it's heavy stuff
Plowing your way from page to page
And prodding your memory to gorge.
History I picked up in scraps;
Never had the time for more.
And then, of course, for the evil days
One needs a faith in something sure—
So I took religion, in little sips;
It goes down easier that way.
Study should not be omnivorous,
But strictly with an eye to use——

COTTON

Now that's practical!

PEER GYNT (*lighting a cigar*)
　　　　　　　　Dear friends,
Consider the career I've traced.
What was I when I headed west?
A ragged boy with empty hands.
I had to grub hard for everything,
And, believe me, I came near despair.
But life, my friends, life is dear,
And death, as they say, has a sting.
Well! Luck, as you know, was kind to me;
And old Fate showed liberality.
Things moved. I took them flexibly
And, step by step, rose up the ladder.
Within ten years I bore the name
Of Croesus with the Charleston traders.

Port after port declared my fame,
And fortune rode in all my hulls——

COTTON
　　What was the trade?

PEER GYNT
　　　　　　　　I made deals
Mainly in slaves for the Carolinas
And idols I marketed in China.

BALLON
　　Fi donc!

TRUMPETERSTRAALE
　　　　By thunder, Uncle Gynt!

PEER GYNT
No doubt you feel that, morally,
Traffic like that had a certain taint?
I know the feeling thoroughly.
I, too, found it odious.
But, as you know, a good investment
Isn't so easily shaken loose.
And then it's especially difficult
In such a prodigious operation
That places thousands of men in motion,
Once and for all, to call a halt.
That "once and for all" I never could stand;
But I will admit, on the other hand,
That I've always nourished a respect
For what they call the consequences;
Crossing the bounds of common sense is
Something that leaves me feeling spooked.
Then, besides, I was getting on—
The last of my forties running out,
And my hair shot through with graying streaks.
My health remained exceptional,
But a thought kept throbbing in my skull:
"Who knows how soon the hour may strike
When the great judgment's handed down
That parts forever the sheep and goats."
　　What to do? To end the trade

With China was unthinkable.
I saw the answer, pushed ahead
With another line of exportables.
In the spring I sent out idols still—
But added missionaries in the fall,
Providing them with all their needs,
Like stockings, Bibles, rum, and rice——

COTTON
    At a profit?

PEER GYNT
                Why, naturally, yes.
Things moved. They worked like mad.
For every idol sale we closed,
They got a coolie well baptized;
The result—an equilibrium.
The missions never lacked for work;
The idols came in a steady stream,
And the preachers held them right in check.

COTTON
    But what about the African wares?

PEER GYNT
    Triumph again for my moral code.
I realized that the trade was bad
For a person of advancing age;
Death might suddenly give a nudge.
Then, too, there were a thousand snares
Laid by the philanthropic boys,
As well as the hostile privateers,
The risk of reefs and angry seas—
All these together made my choice.
I thought: ah, Peter, furl your sails,
Mend your errors, prune your goals.
So I bought a piece of land down south,
Held back the last transport of meat,
Which turned out prime, a perfect lot.
They flourished well, fat and glossy,
Which tickled them as much as me.
Yes, I'll tell you the sober truth:
I was like a father to them——

And, sure enough, the profits came.
I built them schools entrusted with
The central task of keeping virtue
At a certain uniform *niveau*
And watched its temperature like a hawk
So it wouldn't waver from the mark.
Now, moreover, I've resigned
From that whole phase of my career—
I've sold off the plantation and
All the livestock, hide and hair.
On leaving, I rolled out the keg,
And young and old had gratis grog;
The men, the women, all got stiff—
And the widows reveled in my snuff.
So now I hope—provided that
It's not untrue what I've heard said:
"Do no evil, and you've done some good—"
That my mistakes will fade from sight,
And, more than most, I'll find a rinse
Of virtue will dissolve my sins.

EBERKOPF (*clinking glasses with him*)
How inspiriting to hear
A master principle worked out,
Freed from theoretic doubt,
Unshaken by the world's uproar!

PEER GYNT (*who has, through the above, been steadily
　　pulling at the bottle*)
We northmen, we know how to bear
A battle through! Yes, the key
To the art of living—it's to find
Some way of sealing off the mind
From the serpent with the glittering eye.

COTTON
What do you mean by serpent, friend?

PEER GYNT
A little one, one that can twist
A man to whatever is hard and fast.

　　　　　　(*Drinks again.*)

What's the art of daring, of
Courage in action, what is it,
But to move with uncommitted feet
Among the tricky snares of life—
To know for sure that all your days
Aren't over on the day you fight—
To know that behind you always lies
A bridge secured for your retreat.
This policy has built my name
And colored all I've consummated.
It's something I inherited
From the people of my childhood home.

BALLON
  You're Norwegian?

PEER GYNT
              By birth! But a
Citizen of the world by creed.
For the good fortune I've enjoyed,
I have to thank America.
I've drawn my library of books
From the latest German scholars' works.
From France, I took a taste in dress,
My manners and my turn of wit—
From England, enterprising spirit
And an eye for my own advantages.
The Jews have taught me how to wait.
From Italy, I gained a bit
Of a flair for *dolce far niente*—
And once, when events were violently
Disposed, I stretched my years no small
Amount with the aid of Swedish steel.

TRUMPETERSTRAALE (*raising his glass*)
  Ah, Swedish steel—!

EBERKOPF
              A toast instead
To the man of steel who swung the blade!

      (*They clink glasses and drink with*
      PEER, *who begins to show the wine.*)

COTTON
> What you've been saying's very nice—
> But now, sir, I'm most curious
> About your plans for all your treasure.

PEER GYNT (*smiling*)
> Hm—plans? What—?

ALL FOUR (*edging closer*)
>   Yes, let's hear!

PEER GYNT
> Well, first of all, to make a tour.
> That's why I asked you gentlemen on
> To keep me company at Gibraltar.
> I needed friends to dance a tune
> For the golden calf on his seagoing altar.

EBERKOPF
> Neatly put!

COTTON
>   But nobody stirs
> From port only to take a sail.
> You've got some project, I can tell.
> And that project is——

PEER GYNT
>   To be emperor.

ALL FOUR
> What?

PEER GYNT (*nodding*)
>   Emperor!

ALL FOUR
>   Where?

PEER GYNT
>   The whole world.

BALLON
> But how, my friend—?

PEER GYNT

　　　　　　　　　The power of money!
The idea hasn't just entered my head;
It's been the soul of all I've willed.
As a boy in dreams I used to journey
Over the ocean on a cloud.
I floated with cape and golden scabbard—
Then fell down, barking my elbows hard.
But, friends, my will has never swayed—
It's been written or else been said
Someplace, I can't remember where,
That if you won the earth entire
And *lost your self*,[34] what would you gain
But a wreath on a grinning skeleton.
That's the text—approximately;
And it's a lot more truth than poetry.

EBERKOPF

But what, then, is this Gyntian self?

PEER GYNT

The world behind my brow that serves
To set me as far from anyone else
As God's grace from the devil's wiles.

TRUMPETERSTRAALE

Now I see what you're driving at!

BALLON

Sublime thinker!

EBERKOPF

　　　　　　Exalted poet!

PEER GYNT (*with rising emotion*)

The Gyntian self—it's an army corps
Of wishes, appetites, desires.
The Gyntian self is a churning sea
Of whims, demands, necessities—
In short, whatever moves my soul
And makes me live to *my* own will.
But just as our Lord had need of clay
To be creator of the universe,
So I need gold if I'm to play

The emperor's part with any force.

BALLON
But you have the gold!

PEER GYNT
                    Not enough.
Oh yes, for a three-day wonder child,
An emperor à la Lippe-Detmold.[35]
But I have to be, en bloc, *myself*,
A name in every country known—
Sir Peter Gynt from heel to crown.

BALLON (*enraptured*)
And own the most exquisite beauty!

EBERKOPF
Johannisberger, cellars full!

TRUMPETERSTRAALE
And Charles the Twelfth's [36] whole arsenal!

COTTON
But first, find an opportunity
For profit——

PEER GYNT
                    All provided for.
It's the reason why we anchored here.
Tonight we lay a course northeast.
Those papers brought on board were spiced
With news that's quickened my resolve.

                    (*Rises, lifting his glass.*)

It seems that Fortune finds it normal
To help the man who helps himself——

THE FOUR
Well? Tell us—!

PEER GYNT
                    Greece is in turmoil.

ALL FOUR (*springing up*)
What! The Greeks—?

PEER GYNT

                    Are out to fight.

ALL FOUR
  Hurray!

PEER GYNT

          And the Turks are in a sweat!

          (*Drains his glass.*)

BALLON
  To Hellas—and honor! I'll take a chance
  And help them—with French armaments!

EBERKOPF
  I'll do what I can—on long-term notes!

COTTON
  And I too—at low interest rates!

TRUMPETERSTRAALE
  Lead on! In Bender [37] let me find
  Those buckles King Charles left behind!

BALLON (*embracing* PEER GYNT)
  My friend, forgive me; for a while
  I misjudged you!

EBERKOPF (*pressing his hands*)
                  And I'm a fool;
  I'd found you almost contemptible!

COTTON
  That's too strong. Just rather simple——

TRUMPETERSTRAALE (*trying to kiss him*)
  And I had you marked for an example
  Of the cheapest kind of Yankee rabble.
  Forgive me—!

EBERKOPF

              We've all been led astray——

PEER GYNT
  What do you mean?

EBERKOPF
<blockquote>Now we can see
The thronging splendor of that army corps
Of Gyntian wishes and desires——!</blockquote>

BALLON (*admiringly*)
<blockquote>So *this* is being a Gynt, monsieur!</blockquote>

EBERKOPF (*in the same tone*)
<blockquote>No less than being a man of honor!</blockquote>

PEER GYNT
<blockquote>Speak out——</blockquote>

BALLON
<blockquote>You don't understand?</blockquote>

PEER GYNT
<blockquote>Hang me, but I'm in the dark!</blockquote>

BALLON
<blockquote>Why so? Aren't you off to lend
Your ship and money to the Greeks?</blockquote>

PEER GYNT (*snorting*)
<blockquote>Oh, no thanks! My money backs
The side of might; and that's the Turks.</blockquote>

BALLON
<blockquote>Absurd!</blockquote>

EBERKOPF
<blockquote>Amusing, for a joke!</blockquote>

PEER GYNT (*is briefly silent, then leans against a chair
and assumes a superior look*)
<blockquote>Listen, gentlemen, it's best
We separate before the rest
Of our friendship blows away like smoke.
A man with next to nothing favors
Risk; if he owns no more of earth
Than the strip of ground his shadow covers,
He'll fling his life in the cannon's mouth.
But when your fat's well out of the fire,
As mine is, then the stakes are higher.</blockquote>

Go on to Greece. I'll gladly arm
You gratis and put you safe ashore.
The more you fan the flames of war,
The more propitious for my terms.
Strike for freedom and for right!
Smite the Turk! Pour on the heat—
Till all your blood and glory drenches
Down the janissary lances—
But excuse me out.

(*Slaps his pocket.*)

                    That's all I want—
Money! And myself, Sir Peter Gynt!

(*Puts up his sunshade and goes into the
grove where the hammocks can be seen.*)

TRUMPETERSTRAALE
The swine!

BALLON

                No respect for honor—!

COTTON
Oh, honor rot! The profits—! When or
Where can we find another chance
Like this, if they win independence——

BALLON
I saw myself in triumph, hidden
By wreaths of beautiful Greek maidens!

TRUMPETERSTRAALE
There, in my Swedish hands, I saw
Those great, heroic buckles glow!

EBERKOPF
And I saw my fatherland's *Kultur*
Advancing on every foreign shore!

COTTON
We've lost the most financially.
Goddam! [38] So help me, I could cry!
I saw Olympus all my own;

And if that mountain's what they say
There ought to be some copper mines
Still reworkable today.
And the Castalia,[39] that stream
That's talked about so much, with all
Its falls—an engineer could pull
Some thousand horsepower out of them——

TRUMPETERSTRAALE

I'm going anyway! My Swedish
Sword's worth more than Yankee cash!

COTTON

Perhaps. But fighting in the line,
Plunged in those multitudes, we'd drown;
And then what profits would we have?

BALLON

Dommage! So near to Fortune's lap—
Now to be stranded on her grave!

COTTON (*shaking his fist at the yacht*)
And locked up in that coffin ship,
The gold he sweated from his blacks—!

EBERKOPF

A master stroke! Come on—! Quick!
His empire hasn't got a prayer!

BALLON

What are you doing?

EBERKOPF

                    Seizing power!
The crew can easily be bought.
On board! I annex the yacht!

COTTON

You—what—?

EBERKOPF

                    Give it my protection!

                    (*Goes to the jolly boat.*)

COTTON
  Self-interest tells me I should give
  A share of that.

> (*Follows* EBERKOPF.)

TRUMPETERSTRAALE
                  Just like a thief!

BALLON
  A shameful business——! But——*enfin!*

> (*Follows after.*)

TRUMPETERSTRAALE
  I'll have to go——but, understand,
  I protest this act to all mankind——!

> (*Joins the others.*)

SCENE   TWO

Another part of the coast. Moonlight and driving clouds. In the far distance, the yacht sails under full steam. PEER GYNT *comes running along the beach. He pinches himself on the arm, then stares out over the sea.*

PEER GYNT
  Nightmares——! Phantoms——! I have to wake up!
  She's put to sea! At a furious clip——!
  Just phantoms! I'm sleeping! Drunk! Or mad!

> (*Wringing his hands.*)

Impossible that I'm left for dead!

> (*Tearing his hair.*)

A dream! I will it to be a dream!
It's terrible! Oh, but it's true, I'm afraid!
My jackass friends——! Hear me, oh God!
Thou righteous and wise——judgment on them——!

(*Reaching up his arms.*)

It's *me*, Peer Gynt! Are you listening, Lord?
Look after me, Father; let me be spared!
Make them turn back! Or lower the gig!
Stop thief! Oh, let the boilers clog!
Please——! Don't fuss with the world's affairs!
It'll manage itself for a while——
Damned if he's listening! Deaf as usual!
That's nice! A God that can't answer prayers!

(*Beckoning upward.*)

Hsst! I'm rid of the slave plantation!
Look what I did for the China missions!
One good turn, now isn't it worth
Another? Help me——!

(*A sheet of flame leaps up from the yacht, followed
by thick, billowing smoke, then the dull boom of
an explosion.* PEER GYNT *lets out a shriek and drops
to the sand. Gradually the smoke clears. The yacht
has vanished.* PEER *is hushed and pale.*)

The sword of wrath!
To the bottom, sunk—every man and mouse!
What a lucky chance! Oh, infinite praise——

(*With emotion.*)

To chance? No, it was more than that.
I was fated to live, and they were not.
All thanks to Thee, who steadfastly loved
And shielded me, in spite of my sins——

(*Draws a deep breath.*)

What a feeling of peace and confidence
To know I was singled out to be saved.
But the desert! What will I drink and eat?
Oh, I'll find something. He'll provide.
Nothing to fear——

(*In a loud, wheedling tone.*)

He wouldn't let
A poor little sparrow like me go unfed!
Be humble in spirit. And learn to wait.
Trust in the Lord with a will of iron—

(*Springs to his feet in terror.*)

That noise in the brush, was that a lion?

(*His teeth chattering.*)

No, that was no lion.

(*Mustering courage.*)

A lion, all right!
Those animals, they go their own way.
They don't bite their betters. They rely
On instinct; they can feel, for instance,
That it's dangerous playing with elephants.
All the same—I could do with a tree.
Over there, those acacias and palms;
I could climb up and have security—
Especially if I knew a few psalms—

(*Clambers up.*)

"Morning and evening are not alike—" [40]
Now that verse has often been analyzed.

(*Settles himself comfortably.*)

How delightful to feel one's soul upraised.
To think nobly is more than to get rich quick.
Trust all to Him. He knows just how high
He can fill my cup with bitter blight.
He does have a fatherly interest in me—

(*Glances out to sea and breathes with a sigh.*)

But economical—that He's not!

S C E N E   T H R E E

Night. A Moroccan camp on the edge of the desert.
Watch fires and lounging soldiers.

A SLAVE (*runs in and tears his hair*)
    He's gone! The Emperor's white charger, gone!

ANOTHER SLAVE (*runs in and rends his garments*)
    The Emperor's sacred robes are stolen!

MOORISH CAPTAIN (*coming up*)
    Find them, or a hundred blows will fall on
    The miserable foot soles of every man!

> (*The soldiers mount horse and gallop*
>   *off in all directions.*)

S C E N E   F O U R

Daybreak. The grove of acacias and palms. Up in
his tree, PEER GYNT, *with a broken branch in his*
hand, is beating off a pack of monkeys.

PEER GYNT
    Wretched! A most disagreeable night.

> (*Striking about him.*)

You back again? Hell's bells,
They're throwing fruit! No, it's something else—
Monkeys, ugh! Disgusting brutes!
"Watch and fight," as the Scripture says,
But how can I, when I'm dull and weary.

> (*Freshly attacked; loses patience.*)

I'll put a crimp in their repertory!
Let me get hold of one of those boys,
Hang him, skin him, and worm inside

Whatever's left of his shaggy hide,
So the others honor the family ties—
What is man anyway? Only a mote.
Fashion and custom can guide us a bit—
Still they come on! Swarming like locusts.
Get away! Shoo! The gibbering fools.
Oh, if I only had a false tail—
Something so I'd resemble the beasts—
Now what? That pattering overhead—!

(*Looking up.*)

An old one—brandishing filth in his paws—!

(*Crouches apprehensively and remains still for a time. The ape makes a gesture;* PEER GYNT *starts coaxing him, as if he were a dog.*)

Ah—there's a boy, good old Bus!
He's reasonable. And perfectly bred.
Would he throw—? No, not on your life—
It's me! Pip-pip! We're the best of friends!
Ai-ai! There now, he understands.
Bus and I, why, we're relatives—[41]
Bus can have sugar tomorrow—! The beast!
The whole load on top of me! Ugh, horrible—!
Or could it be food? It tastes—equivocal;
But then, it's habit that forms our taste.
Who was that thinker, the one who wrote:
"Spit, and trust to the force of habit"—?
Hi, now the young!

(*Striking about.*)

                But this is crazy,
That man, who's lord of this universe,
Should have to put up with—! Help! Mercy!
The old one's foul, but the children are worse!

SCENE FIVE

Early morning. A rocky ground overlooking the desert. On one side, a cleft in the rocks and a cave. A THIEF *and a* FENCE *in the cleft with the Emperor's horse and robes. The horse, richly caparisoned, stands tied to a stone. Riders can be seen far off.*

THE THIEF
The tongues of the lances
Flicker and flash—
See, see!

THE FENCE
They lick at my head—
I feel them slash!
Woe, woe!

THE THIEF (*folding his arms across his chest*)
My father stole;
His son must steal.

THE FENCE
My father received;
I receive as well.

THE THIEF
You must bear your lot;
Be the self you were taught.

THE FENCE (*listening*)
Steps in the thicket!
Away! But where?

THE THIEF
The cavern is deep,
And the Prophet near!

(*They flee, leaving their stolen goods. The riders vanish in the distance.* PEER GYNT *comes in, cutting himself a reed pipe.*)

PEER GYNT

How fresh the morning is! How mild!
The scarab's rolling his ball in the dust;
The snail pokes out of his shell to feast.
Morning! Yes, it's the purest gold—
Just think what marvelous potency
Nature gave to the light of day.
You feel so safe—your courage swells—
You could easily wrestle a couple of bulls—
How peaceful! Oh, the country joys—
Strange I never felt them before;
Why be penned in some crowded place,
Victim to every knock at the door—?
Ah, look at the lizards whisking their tails,
Snapping and thinking of nothing at all.
What innocence the animals have!
They each obey the Creator's will,
Hold their own features immutable,
Are themselves, themselves through joy and strife
Just as they were when He first said, "Live!"

(*Puts on his pince-nez.*)

A toad—in a sandstone block. The rough
Stone frames him in. Only his face is
Showing. The way he sits and gazes
At the world and is to himself—enough—

(*Reflectively.*)

Enough! Himself—? Now where's that from?
It must be some classic I read it in.
The prayer book was it? Or Proverbs then?
Maddening, how with passing time
My memory for dates and places dims.

(*Sits down in the shade.*)

Here's a cool spot for tired feet.
And look, ferns growing. Edible roots.

(*Eats a little.*)

This food's better fit for an animal—
But it's written, "Our nature must be molded."

And elsewhere, "Pride must have a fall."
And, "He who's humbled shall be exalted."

(*Uneasily.*)

Exalted? For me it will happen too—
There's just no other way. It's destined.
Fate will lead me out of this land
And guide my fortunes safely through.
This all is a trial, but I'll be saved—
If only, God willing, my health's preserved.

(*Shakes off such thoughts, lights a cigar,
stretches out, and surveys the desert.*)

What an immense, unbounded waste—
There in the distance, an ostrich strides—
What can one think was really God's
Meaning in these endless miles of dust?
This desert, lacking all sources of life;
This burnt-out cinder on the world's roof—
This patch on the map, forever blank;
This corpse since the dawn of time, that won't
Give its Maker so much as thanks—
Why was it formed—? Nature's extravagant.
Is that the sea eastward, that shimmering streak?
No, it can't be. That's a mirage.
The sea's to the west behind my back,
Dammed out from the plain by a sloping ridge.

(*A thought flashes through him.*)

Dammed out? Then I could—! The hills are small.
Dammed out! A cut, that's it; a canal—
Like a river of life, the waters would run
In through the channel and flood the plain!
Soon all this furnace of sand and rock
Would be as fresh as a rippling lake.
Oases would rise like desert isles,
Atlas turn green like our mountain coasts;
White sails would skim, like wind-blown gulls,
Southward where once the caravans passed.
Quickening breezes would scatter the fumes
Of decay, and dew would drop from the sky;

Men would come building city on city,
And grass would grow beneath the palms.
Beyond the Sahara the country south
Will be the new cradle of human growth.
Factories will hum in Timbuktu;
Bornu [42] will soon be colonized, while
Up through Habes [43] explorers will go
By sleeping car to the Upper Nile.
In the midst of my sea, on a rich oasis,
I'll reproduce the Nordic races.
The dalesman's blood is royal almost;
Arabian crossings will do the rest.
Within a cove, on a shelving strand,
I'll found Peeropolis and reign.
The world's obsolete! Now it's time
For Gyntiana,[44] my virgin land!

(Springs up.)

Only the capital; then it's set—
A key of gold for the ocean's gate!
A crusade against Death! Let the grim miser
Spill the sack where he hoards his treasure.
In every country, freedom burns—
Like the ass in the ark,[45] I'll send a cry
Round the world and baptize in liberty
The bright shores, dreaming in their chains.
Capital! Raise it! Find a source—!
My kingdom—no, half of it—for a horse! [46]

(The horse whinnies among the rocks.)

A horse! Clothing—! Jewels—! And a sword!

(Going closer.)

It can't be! But, yes—! Faith is a force,
A mover of mountains, that I've heard—
But, that it also can move a horse—?
Pah! The fact is, the horse is real—
Ab esse ad posse et cetera,[47] as well—

(Puts on the robes and regards himself.)

Sir Peter—and Turk from head to toe!
How life provides if you give it a chance—
Come on, Grane, up we go!

(*Climbs into the saddle.*)

And under my feet, gold stirrups now—!
Great men show in the style of their mounts!

(*Gallops off into the desert.*)

S C E N E   S I X

The tent of an Arab chief, in an oasis. PEER GYNT,
*in his eastern dress, reclines on cushions. He is
drinking coffee and smoking a long pipe.* ANITRA
*and a company of girls are dancing and singing
to him.*

CHORUS OF GIRLS
The Prophet has come!
The Prophet, the Lord, the All-knowing Mind,
Has come to us riding, to us has come
Over the ocean of sand!
The Prophet, the Lord, the Unfailing One,
Has come to us sailing, to us has come
Over the rolling dunes!
    Sound the flute and the drum;
The Prophet, the Prophet has come!

ANITRA
His steed is like milk, the purest white
That streams in the rivers of Paradise.
Bend your knee! Cover your face!
His eyes are stars, tenderly lit.
No child of clay can endure
The rays of their heavenly fire.
    Out of the desert he came.
Gold and pearls blazed on his chest.
When he rode by, the sunlight passed.
Behind him fled night,

Simoon and drought.
He, the All-glorious, came!
Out of the desert he came,
Dressed like a son of man.
Kaaba [48] now gapes like a tomb—
He has enlightened his own!

CHORUS OF GIRLS
    Sound the flute and the drum;
The Prophet, the Prophet has come!

      (*They dance on to quiet music.*)

PEER GYNT
I've read it in print—and I'll be bound,
"No man's a prophet in his native land."
All this pleases me much better
Than life among the Charleston traders.
There was something hollow in that affair,
Some worm at the root, something queer—
I never could feel myself at home,
Never really fit in with them.
What did I ever want in that crew,[49]
Routing around in the bins of trade?
When I think it all over, I hardly know—
It happened, that's all; so let it ride.
    To be yourself on a base of gold
Is a way of building your house on sand.
For a watch and a ring, the wealth you wield,
The people grovel and lick your hand;
They tip their hats to a diamond pin,
But the ring and stickpin aren't the man—
A prophet! That has a lot more point.
There, at least, you know your place.
If you're taken up, it's *yourself* they praise,
Yourself, and not your bank account.
You are what you are, and no mistake;
Nothing is owed to chance or luck;
No propping yourself with patents and grants—
A prophet! It's really the thing for me.
And to think it took me so unawares—
I was simply crossing the desert here

And these children of nature barred the way.
Their prophet had come; they made that clear.
I really didn't try to deceive—
You can't call lies what a prophet swears;
Besides, you know, I can always leave.
It could be worse; I'm not tied down—
The thing, so to speak, is just between us;
I can go as I came; I have my horse;
In short, I'm on top of the situation.

ANITRA (*approaching*)
Prophet and Lord!

PEER GYNT

Yes, my slave?

ANITRA
The sons of the desert are nearing thy tent;
They ask a glimpse of thy features——

PEER GYNT

Stop!
At a distance, tell them to muster up.
At a distance, let them be reverent.
And add, no man may enter this grove!
Men, child, are a slippery batch—
Low-minded, itchy-fingered, wild—!
Anitra, you couldn't guess how much
They've swind—I mean, have sinned, my child—
Enough of that! Dance, my maidens!
The Prophet would ease his heavy burdens.

THE GIRLS (*dancing*)
The Prophet is good; his heart is grieved
By the evil the sons of dust have loved!
The Prophet is mild; for this, all praise;
He raises sinners to Paradise!

PEER GYNT (*his eyes following* ANITRA *in her dance*)
Her legs go quicker than drumsticks.
Ah, she's a tasty dish, the minx!
Her figure has some extravagant forms—
Hardly in line with beauty's norms;
But then, what's beauty? Convention's choice—

A coin made current by time and place.
It's such extravagance that enchants
Whenever the normal pattern palls.
Within the law, all passion chills.
They're either too stout, or else too gaunt,
Way underage, or shriveled to bone—
And insipid in between—
  Her feet, they're not entirely clean;
Same with the arms; especially the one.
But that's no cause to be critical.
In fact, it's one morsel of her appeal—
  Anitra, hear me!

ANITRA (*approaching*)
      Thy handmaiden hears!

PEER GYNT
 Child, you're bewitching! Lo, you inspire
 The Prophet. If you doubt me, consider this:
 I'll make you a houri in Paradise!

ANITRA
 Impossible, Lord!

PEER GYNT
     Would I deceive?
 I'm dead serious, sure as I live!

ANITRA
 But I have no soul.

PEER GYNT
     It's what you'll get!

ANITRA
 But how, my Lord?

PEER GYNT
     I'll see to that—
 I'm taking over your education.
 No soul? Yes, you are rather dumb;
 It's struck me, with a certain depression.
 But, for a soul, there's always room.
 Come here! Let me measure your braincase—
 There's room, room enough; I *knew* there was.

It's true—you aren't ever going to go
Very deep; a *large* soul isn't for you—
But, after all, what's the difference—
You'll have enough for all your wants——

ANITRA

   The Prophet is kind——

PEER GYNT

            You hesitate? Well!

ANITRA

   But I'd rather have——

PEER GYNT

            Come on, speak out!

ANITRA

   When it comes to a soul, I think I can wait
   But give me——

PEER GYNT

       What?

ANITRA (*points at his turban*)
           That pretty opal!

PEER GYNT (*enraptured, giving her the jewel*)
   Anitra! Child! Eve's own daughter!
   Like a magnet drawing me—for I'm a man;
   And it's just as he said, that famous writer:
   "*Das Ewig-Weibliche zieht uns an!*" [50]

SCENE SEVEN

A moonlit night. The palm grove outside ANITRA'S
tent. PEER GYNT, *with an Arabian lute in hand, sits
under a tree. His beard and hair have been
trimmed; he looks noticeably younger.*

PEER GYNT (*plays and sings*)
   I locked away my paradise
   And carried off the key,

Sailed out before the northern breeze,
While lovely ladies spent their cries
Forlornly by the sea.

Southward, southward raced the keel
Across the ocean stream.
Where palm trees swaying proud and tall
Around a bay stood sentinel,
I put my ship to flame.

I climbed aboard the desert ship,
A ship on four swift legs.
It foamed beneath the lashing whip;
Oh, catch me on the wing! I slip,
A songbird, through the twigs!

Anitra! Nectar of the palm
Is how I see thee now!
Angora goat cheese in its prime
Gives hardly half so sweet a balm,
Anitra, dear, as thou!

(*Hangs the lute over his shoulder
and approaches the tent.*)

Silence! Did my beauty listen?
What did she think of my little song?
Is she peeping behind the curtain,
Stripped of her veils and everything?
What's that? Sounds like somebody tore
A cork from a bottle violently!
Again? And again! What could it be?
Sighs, perhaps? Love's melody—
No, that was a definite snore—
Sweetest music! Anitra sleeps.
Nightingale, be muted now!
You'll get your money's worth in woe
If you dare mingle your raucous pipes—
Oh well, as the book says, let it go!
The nightingale is a troubadour;
And, for all that, so am I.
Both of us with our music snare

Hearts that are tender, mild, and shy.
The cool of night is made for singing;
Song defines our common role.
Song is our way of remaining
Us, Peer Gynt and the nightingale.
And just this, my beauty there asleep,
Is the crowning bliss of love—
No more; only to touch my lip
To the cup, and leave the nectar safe—
But look, she's coming out at last!
Well, after all, that is the best.

ANITRA (*from the tent*)
Lord, were you calling in the night?

PEER GYNT
Yes, I was; that was the Prophet.
I was awakened by the cat
Out hunting, with an awful racket——

ANITRA
Those weren't the sounds of hunting, Lord;
It was something worse you heard.

PEER GYNT
What was it, then?

ANITRA
                    Oh, spare me!

PEER GYNT
                              Tell!

ANITRA
Oh, I'm blushing——

PEER GYNT (*coming closer*)
                    Could it have been
That feeling that suffused me when
I made you a present of my opal?

ANITRA (*horrified*)
You put yourself, oh earth's delight,
On a par with an old disgusting cat!

PEER GYNT

    Child, in love's delirium,
    A prophet and a tomcat come
    Out to very much the same.

ANITRA

    Lord, from your lips diversion flows
    Like beads of honey.

PEER GYNT

               Little one—
    You, like other girls, appraise
    Only the surfaces of great men.
    Inside me, comedy runs wild,
    Especially when we're alone like this.
    In my position, I'm compelled
    To mask it under seriousness.
    The day's routine is a heavy weight;
    All the worry and distress
    That comes to me on every face
    Makes me prophetically morose;
    But only from the surface out—
    No more! Away! In a tête-à-tête,
    I'm what I've always been—I'm Peer.
    Hi, the prophet gets his hat;
    He's gone! Myself, you have me here!

        (*Sits under a tree and draws her to him.*)

    Come, Anitra, rest a while
    Under the palm tree's emerald fan.
    Let me whisper to your smile;
    Later we'll change roles, and then
    I'll lie and smilingly approve
    Your fresh, young lips that whisper love.

ANITRA (*stretching out at his feet*)

    Each word you speak is sweet as a bell;
    I wish I followed the meaning better.
    Master, tell me, can your daughter,
    Just by listening, gain a soul?

PEER GYNT

    The spirit's light and truth, a soul—

Yes, you'll gain one after a spell.
When the rose-streaked east horizon
Reads, in gold print—"Now it's day"—
Then, my mouse, you'll have your lesson;
Then you'll be tutored properly.
But in the night's enchanted calm
It would be stupid if my aim
Were only with some worn-out tags
Of learning to play pedagogue.
In our lives, the soul is—once
You see it rightly—not the key.
It's the heart that really counts.

ANITRA

Speak, oh Master! In your meaning
Now I see light, like opals shining!

PEER GYNT

Too much shrewdness ends in folly;
The fruit of fear is cruelty;
Truth in exaggeration can
Be wisdom written upside down.
Yes, my child—I'd take my oath
And swear that there's a certain class
Of soul-inflated folk on earth
Who won't reach clarity with ease.
I knew a fellow just like that,
The finest flower of the lot;
But even he mistook the goal
And lost his purpose, spinning wool—
Around this grove, you see the wastes?
If I were to swing my turban wide,
I could make all the ocean's flood
Sweep in and drown these miles of dust.
But I'd be one of the half-baked minds
If I went about making seas and lands.
Tell me, do you know what it is to live? [51]

ANITRA
Teach me that!

PEER GYNT

It's simply to move

Dryshod down the stream of time,
Oneself, intact, above all claims.
Only in fullest manhood can I
Be what I am, my dearest joy!
The old eagles shed their feathers,
The old veterans drag their breath,
The old fishwives lose their teeth,
The old hands of the misers wither;
All of them wither in their souls—
Youth! Oh, youth! I want to reign
Like a sultan, fiery in my pulse—
Not on Gyntiana's shores
In her vine and palm-tree arbors—
But sovereign of a fresher green,
The world of a maiden's pure desires.
　　Now do you see, my little one,
Why I've graciously paid you court—
Why I singled out your heart
To be, as it were, the foundation stone
Of all my being's caliphate?
Over your longings, I'll be lord.
In passion, I'm an autocrat!
You have to live for me alone.
I'll be always there to guard
Your charms like a jeweled cameo.
If we should part, life is over—
Nota bene, meaning for *you!*
I want your every inch and fiber
Drained of will and, utterly
Past resistance, filled with me.
Your nest of midnight hair, your skin,
Everything lovely one could name,
Will, like the gardens of Babylon,
Draw your sultan to his true home.
　　So it's fortunate, after all,
Your head is so largely vacuous.
People who entertain a soul
Get swallowed in self-consciousness.
Listen, while we're on this thing—
If you like, by heaven! I'll endow
Your beauty with an ankle ring—

It'll be best for both of us, too,
If *I'm* installed where your soul belongs—
As for the rest—it's *status quo*.

(ANITRA *snores*.)

What? Asleep! Has it gone gliding
Past her, everything I've said?
No; it shows what a mark I've made,
That she should be wafted into dreams
By what my passionate tongue proclaims.

(*Rises and lays jewels in her lap.*)

Take these jewels! And here, some more!
Sleep, Anitra! Dream of Peer—
Dream on! Your sleep has set a crown
Upon the emperor of your thoughts!
By force of character alone
Peer Gynt's won victory tonight.

SCENE EIGHT

A caravan route. The oasis far off in the distance.
PEER GYNT, *on his white horse, comes galloping
across the desert, with* ANITRA *in front on his saddle-
bow.*

ANITRA
Let go; I'll bite!

PEER GYNT
                You little mischief!

ANITRA
What is this game?

PEER GYNT
                The hawk and the dove.
I'll abduct you! Play mad tricks!

ANITRA
Shame! An old prophet—!

PEER GYNT

Ridiculous—
The prophet isn't old, you goose!
Is this a role that old age picks?

ANITRA

Let go! You take me home!

PEER GYNT

Coquette!
Home? To father-in-law? How sweet!
We mad birds that fly our cages
Go where no father-in-law can watch us.
Besides, my child, it never pays
To stay too long in any one place.
What's gained in friendship's lost in esteem—
That's where prophets and such get caught.
You must flash in view, then fade like a dream.
It was time to close the visit out.
The sons of the desert are fickle at heart—
The prayers and incense were running short.

ANITRA

But *are* you a prophet?

PEER GYNT

I'm your emperor!

(*Tries to kiss her.*)

My, how ruffled our feathers are!

ANITRA

Give me that ring there on your finger.

PEER GYNT

Anitra dear, you can have them all!

ANITRA

Your words are songs! They feed my hunger.

PEER GYNT

Bliss, to know that one's loved so well!
Wait! I'll lead the horse, as your slave!

(*Hands her the riding whip and gets off.*)

There, my rosebud, my dainty flower;
I'll push on over the desert, move
Till I drop in this dazzling glare.
I'm young, Anitra; don't forget!
You mustn't be hard on my crazy fits.
Jokes and games are youth's own splendor!
If your mind wasn't such a sluggish thing,
You'd know, my lovely oleander—
That your lover jokes—*ergo*, he's young!

ANITRA

Yes, you're young. The rings, have you more?

PEER GYNT

Aren't I? Here, catch! I can leap like a reindeer!
If I had vineleaves, I'd crown my brow.
Hi, but I'm young! I'm dancing now!

(*Dances and sings.*)

Oh, I'm a happy rooster!
Peck me, my little chick!
Hi! See the footwork, look—
Oh, I'm a happy rooster!

ANITRA

You're sweating, prophet; I'm afraid you'll melt—
Throw me that heavy bag at your belt.

PEER GYNT

What thoughtfulness! Keep it, child—
Hearts full of love can do without gold!

(*Dances and sings again.*)

Young Peer Gynt is a zany—
He doesn't know what foot he's standing on.
Ffft, says Peer—ffft, again—
Young Peer Gynt is a zany!

ANITRA

The prophet, dancing, charms us both!

PEER GYNT

Stow the prophet! Let's change clothes!
Here! Undress!

ANITRA

    Your robe wouldn't fit;
 Your girdle's too big; your stockings, too tight——

PEER GYNT

 Eh bien! (*Kneels.*)
    But give me a piercing sorrow—
 Hearts full of love find suffering sweet!
 And when you enter my castle door, you——

ANITRA

 Your paradise—is it much farther yet?

PEER GYNT

 Oh, a thousand miles——

ANITRA

      Too far!

PEER GYNT

         But wait—
 The soul that I promised you, you'll get——

ANITRA

 Thanks—I'll make it without a soul.
 But you asked for a sorrow——

PEER GYNT (*rising*)

       By heaven, yes!
 Profound, but brief—for a couple of days.

ANITRA

 Anitra obeys the prophet! Farewell!

  (*She cuts him sharply across the knuckles and
   gallops away full tilt across the desert.*)

PEER GYNT (*dumbfounded*)

 Well, I'll be a——

SCENE NINE

The same, an hour later. PEER GYNT, *solemn and
thoughtful, is stripping his Turkish costume off*

piece by piece. Finally he takes his little traveling
cap out of his coat pocket, puts it on, and stands
once more in European dress.

PEER GYNT (*hurling the turban far away*)
　There lies the Turk, and here am I—!
　Heathen existence just doesn't go.
　Lucky it's only the clothes I wore,
　And not burned into me like a scar—
　What did I ever want in that crew?
　It's best to live a Christian life in
　This world, to smother your peacock pride,
　Take law and morality for your guide,
　And be yourself, till at last you're given
　Praise at your grave and wreaths on your coffin.

(*Pacing a few steps.*)

　The minx—she came within a hair
　Of managing to turn my head.
　I'll be a troll if I can figure
　What kind of sorcery she had.
　Ah well, it's done! If I'd let things progress,
　I'd have wound up looking ridiculous.
　I made a mistake. But it's consolation
　That what was wrong was the situation.
　It wasn't the inner man that fell.
　It's this prophetical way of life
　That poisons all that activity heals
　And takes revenge in a cheap rebuff.
　The prophet's role is a sorry show!
　You're mostly groping around in mist;
　And the game is over, the prophet through,
　If he acts at all like a rationalist.
　In *that*, I've only run true to form
　To fall when that goose turned on the charm.
　Still, all the same—

(*Bursts out laughing.*)

　　　　It tickles your fancy!
　To try to stop time by skipping and dancing;
　To fight the current by preening and mincing!

To strum the lute, take love for a fact,
Then end like a hen—by getting plucked.
That's something to call prophetic frenzy—
Plucked! Oh Lord, I've been plucked all right!
Well, it's good that I kept a little out—
Some in America, and some in my pocket;
So I'll not be a beggar sleeping in thickets.
And the middle class, it's really best.
A coach-and-four isn't worth the cost—
Why should I travel like a patrician?
In short, I'm on top of the situation—
Now what should I choose? Such vistas call;
And choice marks the master from the fool.
My business life is a closed book;
My love game is a ragged cloak.
I'm not going crabwise, back again.
"Forward and back, it's just as far;
Out or in, it's a narrow door,"
Was written, I think, by some holy man.
For something new; some flight of valor;
Some end worth every effort and dollar
Spent! If I set my life story down
Complete, for guidance and imitation—?
Or, wait—! I've plenty of time at hand—
What if I went as a wandering scholar
To trace what the past has left behind?
Yes, that's it! There's my place!
I always read legends as a child;
And now, with the sciences I've distilled—
I'll follow the course of the human race!
I'll float like a feather on history's stream,
Relive it all, as if in a dream—
See the heroes battle for truth and right,
But as an onlooker, safe in thought—
See thinkers perish and martyrs bleed,
See empires rise and sweep to doom,
See the world epochs sprout from seed—
In short, I'll skim off history's cream.
I must get hold of a volume of Becker [52]
And travel chronologically secure.
It's true—my groundwork's not very deep,

And history's mazes can be a trap—
But then sometimes the wildest notions
Can lead to original conclusions—
How exalting, to set up a goal
And drive right to it, like flint and steel!

(*With quiet feeling.*)

To break off every tie that binds
One to homeland and to friends—
To blow one's treasured wealth to bits—
Give all to love, then call it quits—
For truth, for light from the ultimate torch—

(*Brushing a tear from his eye.*)

That has the spirit of pure research!
I feel so happy, beyond all measure.
Now I've unriddled my destiny here.
It's just to bear out my predicament—!
I shouldn't be blamed for vanity if
I savor being the man Peer Gynt,
Known as the Emperor of Human Life—
The whole of the past I want to own;
Never come near the living again—
This age isn't worth the heel of my shoe.
Men have no faith, no substance now:
Souls without wings, deeds without weight—

(*Shrugging his shoulders.*)

And the women—pah, they're a slippery lot!

(*Goes off.*)

SCENE TEN

*A summer day in the far north. A hut in the forest.
The door, with its large wooden bar, stands open.
Reindeer horns over the doorway. A flock of goats
by one wall.* A MIDDLD-AGED WOMAN, *fair and still
lovely, sits out in the sunlight, spinning.*

THE WOMAN (*glances down the path and sings*)
    The winter may pass, and the spring turn to air,
    And next summer too, and the whole of the year—
    But one day you'll come, I know that you will;
    Then, true to my promise, I'll wait for you still.

    (*Calls to the goats, spins, and sings again.*)

    God give you strength if you wander alone!
    God give you joy if you stand at His throne!
    I'll wait for you here till you're home again safe;
    And if heaven has you, we'll meet there, my love!

SCENE ELEVEN

Egypt. The statue of Memnon,[53] *in the first light of
dawn, surrounded by desert.* PEER GYNT *approaches
on foot and studies the scene for a while.*

PEER GYNT
    Here's a good spot for the trip to begin—
    Now, for a change, I'll be an Egyptian,
    Founded, that is, on a Gyntian core.
    Then Assyria—I'll go there.
    To start right back at the world's creation
    Would only lead me into confusion—
    I'll skip over Biblical fact and belief;
    Their secular traces will give me enough;
    And to put them under hard scrutiny
    Is neither my plan nor facility.

    (*Sitting on a rock.*)

    Now let me rest and quietly wait
    Till the statue's morning song floats out.
    Then breakfast; a climb up the pyramid;
    And, if there's time, a look inside.
    Then round the top of the Red Sea shore;
    I might find the grave of King Potiphar—
    Now I'm Asian. I'm searching in Babylon
    For the hanging gardens, the concubines—

The hallmarks of cultured society.
Next, in one bound, to the walls of Troy.
From Troy there's a sea route goes direct
To Athens, queen city of monuments—
There I'll explore the pass that once
Leonidas fought and died to protect—
I'll study the leading philosophers,
Find Socrates' cell, where he ended his years—
Damn! I forgot—there's a war going on—!
Well, Hellenism I'll have to postpone.

(*Looks at his watch.*)

It's really absurd how long it takes
For the sun to rise. I can't waste time.
All right now, Troy—that's as far as I'd come—

(*Gets up and listens.*)

What is it, that curious murmur that breaks—?

(*Sunrise.*)

MEMNON'S STATUE (*sings*)
From the demigod's ashes rise youth-renewing
     birds brightly singing.
     Zeus, the All-knowing,
     made struggle their longing.
     Wise Owl, among
birds, is sleep so much safer?
You must die or decipher
     this riddle in song!

PEER GYNT
Fantastic—I do think the statue expressed
Those sounds! Music, it was, of the past.[54]
I heard the stone voice rising and falling—
I'll put the facts down for future mulling.

(*Writes in his notebook.*)

"The statue sang. Heard definite tones,
But can't quite figure what it all means.

An hallucination, obviously.
Nothing else worthy of note today."

(Moves on.)

S C E N E   T W E L V E

Near the village of Gizeh. The Great Sphinx, carved
out of rock. Far off, the spires and minarets of
Cairo. PEER GYNT *enters; he observes the Sphinx*
with some care, by turns first through his pince-nez
and then through his hollowed hand.

PEER GYNT
Where in the world did I meet up before
With this thing, this nightmare from long ago?
I know we've met—up north, or here.
Was it a person? And, if so, who?
Memnon, it came to me afterwards,
Looked like the King of the Dovre Trolls,
The way he was sitting, stiff as a board,
With pillars propping his bottom like stools—
But this wonder that's neither fish nor fowl,
This freak, this lion and woman joined—
Is it also out of some fairy tale?
Or something real that I've held in mind—?
From a fairy tale? Ho, I remember the brute!
It's the Boyg, of course, whose skull I split—
Or dreamed I did—I was ill of fever—

(Going closer.)

The selfsame eyes; the lips, same as ever—
Not quite so listless, a bit more sly;
But otherwise, one and the same to a tee.
So that's it, Boyg; you look like a lion,
Seen from behind by the light of day.
You still make riddles? We can try one
And see if you measure the same in this too—!

(Calls to the Sphinx.)

Hi, Boyg, who are you?

A VOICE (*behind the Sphinx*)
                    Ach, Sphinx, wer bist du?

PEER GYNT
   What? An echo in German? How odd!

THE VOICE
Wer bist du?

PEER GYNT
            The accent, it's very good!
   A new observation, completely mine.

            (*Writes in his notebook.*)

   "Echo speaks German. Dialect—Berlin."

        (BEGRIFFENFELDT *comes out from behind the
                    Sphinx.*)

BEGRIFFENFELDT
   A man!

PEER GYNT
         So *he's* the explanation.

            (*Notes again.*)

   "Later came to another conclusion."

BEGRIFFENFELDT (*with agitated gestures*)
   Pardon, *mein Herr*—! *Eine Lebensfrage*—!
   What brought you here just at this second?

PEER GYNT
   A visit. I'm greeting a childhood friend.

BEGRIFFENFELDT
   The Sphinx—?

PEER GYNT (*nods*)
            An early page of my saga.

BEGRIFFENFELDT
   Splendid! And this after, ah, what a night!
   My head is throbbing, ready to burst!

You know him? Speak, man! Tell me first
What is he?

PEER GYNT

       What is he? Nothing to that.
He's *himself.*

BEGRIFFENFELDT (*with a bound*)

       The riddle of life, in a blaze
Of light, is clear! You're sure that he *is*
Himself?

PEER GYNT

       Yes; or that's what he says.

BEGRIFFENFELDT

Himself! Revolution, thine hour is close!

       (*Takes off his hat.*)

Your name, *mein Herr?*

PEER GYNT

       I was christened Peer Gynt.

BEGRIFFENFELDT (*with quiet admiration*)

Peer Gynt! Allegorical! Just as I thought—
Peer Gynt? The unknown one, the great
New oracle predicted and sent——

PEER GYNT

No, really! So you're here to invite—?

BEGRIFFENFELDT

Peer Gynt! Profound! Mystical! Robust!
Each word seems part of a vast design!
What are you?

PEER GYNT (*modestly*)

       I've always sought to remain
Myself. My passport covers the rest.

BEGRIFFENFELDT

Again the mysterious phrase intoned!

       (*Seizes his wrist.*)

To Cairo! The Interpreter's Emperor is found!

PEER GYNT
  Emperor?

BEGRIFFENFELDT
          Come!

PEER GYNT
          Have they heard of me?

BEGRIFFENFELDT (*pulling him along*)
  The Interpreter's Emperor—by self's decree!

SCENE THIRTEEN

*In Cairo. A large courtyard enclosed by high walls
and buildings. Barred windows; iron cages.* THREE
KEEPERS *in the yard. A* FOURTH *enters.*

FOURTH KEEPER
  Say, Schafmann, where's the director gone?

FIRST KEEPER
  Went out this morning before it was light.

FOURTH KEEPER
  Something's gotten him all upset;
  Last night——

SECOND KEEPER
          Hsst, quiet; he's coming in!

(BEGRIFFENFELDT *enters, leading* PEER GYNT, *locks
      the gate and puts the key in his pocket.*)

PEER GYNT (*to himself*)
  This man is incredibly talented;
  Nearly all he says is over my head.

          (*Looking about.*)

So here we are, in the Scholar's Club?

BEGRIFFENFELDT
Here's where you'll find them, all that mob—
The threescore and ten Interpreters; [55]
Now raised by a hundred and sixty more—

(*Shouts at the* KEEPERS.)

Mikkel, Schlingelberg, Schafmann, Fuchs—
Into the cages, in just two shakes!

KEEFERS
Us?

BEGRIFFENFELDT
Who else? Come on! Get in!
When the world goes spinning, we have to spin.

(*Forces them into a cage.*)

He came this morning, Peer the Great—
You can guess the rest—I'll leave it at that.

(*Locks the cage and throws the key down a well.*)

PEER GYNT
But Doctor—my dear Herr Director, please——

BEGRIFFENFELDT
Not any more! That's what I *was*—
Can you keep a secret? I have a confession——

PEER GYNT (*increasingly uneasy*)
What's that?

BEGRIFFENFELDT
You think you can stand the shock?

PEER GYNT
Well, I'll try——

BEGRIFFENFELDT (*draws him into a corner and whispers*)
The Absolute Reason
Died last night at eleven o'clock.

PEER GYNT
Good God—!

BEGRIFFENFELDT
                    Yes, it's really deplorable.
And in *my* position, nearly unbearable,
For these grounds have been, up to this time,
An insane asylum.

PEER GYNT
                        An insane asylum!

BEGRIFFENFELDT
  But not any more!

PEER GYNT (*pale and subdued*)
                    Now I know this place!
  The man's gone mad—and nobody knows!

                    (*Moves away.*)

BEGRIFFENFELDT (*following him*)
  I wouldn't want you to misunderstand.
  When I say He's dead—I'm making jokes.
  He's escaped himself. He's come unskinned—
  Just like my countryman Munchausen's fox.[56]

PEER GYNT
  Excuse me——

BEGRIFFENFELDT (*catching hold of him*)
                    He was more like an eel than
  A fox. That's it! Through the eye, a pin—
  He writhed on the wall——

PEER GYNT
                        Oh, save me that—!

BEGRIFFENFELDT
  Round the neck, a slit—and whip! it's out
  Of its skin!

PEER GYNT
        Crazy! He's lost his mind!

BEGRIFFENFELDT
  You can't get away from it; it's clear—
  This escape-from-selfing has to inspire
  Complete revolution in every land.

People who've all been mad as loons
Last night at eleven became quite sane,
Conforming to Reason's latest phase.
And from this standpoint, it's even more
Clear that, at that identical hour,
The so-called sane lost their faculties.

PEER GYNT
You mentioned the hour; my time is short——

BEGRIFFENFELDT
Your time? That gives my memory a spurt!

(Opens a door and calls out.)

Come forth! The age of the future has dawned!
Reason is dead. Long live Peer Gynt!

PEER GYNT
You're much too kind——!

> *(The lunatics come, one after another,*
> *into the courtyard.)*

BEGRIFFENFELDT
                     Good morning! Come,
Greet the ascending orb of freedom!
Your emperor's here!

PEER GYNT
              Emperor?

BEGRIFFENFELDT
                    Yes!

PEER GYNT
But the honor's too much; it's way beyond——

BEGRIFFENFELDT
Ah, false modesty——don't let it bind
This moment.

PEER GYNT
          Give me some peace——!
No, I'm not worthy! What can I say?

BEGRIFFENFELDT

A man who brought the Sphinx to bay?
A man who's himself?

PEER GYNT

But that's just it.
I'm myself in everything I do;
But as far as I can see, here you
Have to be out of yourself to rate.

BEGRIFFENFELDT

Out of yourself? What a huge mistake!
Everyone here is himself to the gills,
Completely himself and nothing else—
So far in himself he can't come back.
Everyone's shut in his cask of skin;
He dives in the self's fermenting murk,
Hermetically sealed by a self-made cork—
Shrinking his staves down a well of brine.
No one has tears for the others' griefs,
Or feels at all for the others' beliefs.
We're ourselves in every thought and tone,
Ourselves to the farthest margin out—
And so, if an emperor on a throne
Is what we need, you're exactly right.

PEER GYNT

Oh, how the devil—!

BEGRIFFENFELDT

Don't feel blue;
Nearly all that is once had to be new.
"Oneself"—here, look, I'll show you a case;
I'll pick at random the first that passes—

(*To a dark figure.*)

Good day, Huhu! [57] Why's there a crisis
Always written across your face?

HUHU

Can I help it when my nation
Dies without interpretation?

(*To* PEER GYNT.)

You're a stranger; will you listen?

PEER GYNT

Why, of course!

HUHU

You'll hear my reason—
Strung like garlands east of here
Lie the coasts of Malabar.
Dutch and Portuguese have seeded
Culture with the goods they traded,
While the jungle hid their quarries—
Droves of native Malabaris.
These get by on hybrid words—
In the backland they're the lords—
But the ages past belong
To the fierce orangoutang.
He, the forest's lord and master,
Free to snarl or pick a blister—
Handsomely he gaped and grinned,
Shaped direct from nature's hand.
Generously he shrieked his fill;
He was monarch over all—
But then foreign sirens sang,
Muddling our primeval tongue,
While four centuries of sleep
Quelled the vigor of the ape—
For, you know, a night like that
Snuffs a people's spirit out.
No more forest cries are heard;
Growls and grunts just go ignored—
If we want to share our views,
Language is the thing to use.
What a plague on every race!
Now the Dutch, the Portuguese,
Malabaris, polyglots—
All get driven into fits.
I must fight to keep in touch
With the old, authentic speech—
Fight to raise its corpse and strike
For the people's right to shriek—
Shriek myself and bring new fire

To the folk songs we admire.
Still, my efforts win no favor—
Now you see the way I suffer.
Thanks for hearing out my reason—
How would you advise me, cousin?

PEER GYNT (*to himself*)
    It's been said: when wolves are howling,
    Then it's wise to do some growling.

(*Aloud.*)

Friend, if I remember right,
In Morocco there's a spot
Where the apes are pining for
Poets and interpreters.
Their tongue sounded Malabarish—
Classic diction with a flourish!
Why don't you, like other gentry,
Emigrate to serve your country?

HUHU
    Thanks for hearing out my reason—
    As you counsel, so I've chosen.

(*With a sweeping gesture.*)

East! Thy bard has suffered wrongs!
West! Thou hast orangoutangs!

(*He goes.*)

BEGRIFFENFELDT
    Well, was he himself? I think he was.
    Completely filled with his own distress.
    Himself in all that his thoughts involve—
    Himself by being out of himself.
    Come here! I'll show you another one
    Who found last night he was truly sane.

(*To a* FELLAH *carrying a mummy on his back.*) [58]

King Apis, how goes my noble lord?

FELLAH (*wildly, to* PEER GYNT)
    Am I King Apis?

PEER GYNT (*shrinking behind the doctor*)
Well, it's hard
To say; I don't know the situation.
But if I were judging by your passion——

FELLAH

Now you're lying too.

BEGRIFFENFELDT

Your Highness should tell
How matters stand.

FELLAH

As you will.

(Turning to PEER GYNT.)

You see him, there on my shoulders?
His name was Apis, the King.
Now he just goes for a mummy,
And he's dead to everything.

   He built the pyramids skyward
And carved out the mighty Sphinx,
And fought, as the Doctor put it,
With the Turk both *rechts* and *links*.

   For this the people of Egypt
Hailed him a god over all,
And raised him up in the temples
In the likeness of a bull.[59]

   But *I* am this same King Apis,
I see that as plain as day;
And if you can't understand me,
I'll clear it up right away.

   King Apis, you see, was out hunting
When he suddenly started to squirm,
And he got off his horse and retired
To part of my ancestor's farm.

   But the field that King Apis manured
Has nourished *me* with its corn;
And if more proof is required,
Well—I have an invisible horn.

   Now isn't it quite outrageous
That no one honors my rights!

By birth, I'm Apis, the pharaoh,
But a fellah in other men's sight.
    If you see my course of action,
Please, put it to me straight—
The thing is, what can I do now
To be like King Apis the Great?

PEER GYNT

Build pyramids, your Highness,
And carve out a mightier Sphinx,
And fight, as the Doctor puts it,
With the Turk both *rechts* and *links*.

FELLAH

Yes, that's very high-spoken!
A fellah! A hungry louse!
It's enough just keeping my hovel
Empty of rats and mice.
    Quick, man—find something better,
A greatness founded on rock
To make me the spitting image
Of Apis here on my back!

PEER GYNT

Your Highness could hang himself,
And through the earth's weathering
And the coffin's natural confines,
Go dead to everything.

FELLAH

I'll do it! My life for a gallows!
A rope to hold my weight!
At first there'll be some difference,
But time will even that out.

                (*Goes off and prepares to hang himself.*)

BEGRIFFENFELDT

Now that's personality, *mein Herr*—
A man of method——

PEER GYNT

                        Oh yes, I'm sure—
But he'll really hang himself! God in heaven!

I feel sick——! My brain's like an oven!

BEGRIFFENFELDT
A state of transition; it won't last long.

PEER GYNT
Transition? To what? Sorry—I'm going——

BEGRIFFENFELDT (*holding him*)
Are you mad?

PEER GYNT
Not yet. Mad? God forbid!

(*Commotion.* HUSSEIN, *a government minister,*[60] *pushes his way through the crowd.*)

HUSSEIN
They tell me an emperor came today.

(*To* PEER GYNT.)

Is it you?

PEER GYNT (*in despair*)
It's turning out that way!

HUSSEIN
Good. You have papers to be drafted?

PEER GYNT (*tearing his hair*)
Yes! Why not? The madder the better!

HUSSEIN
I'd be honored, sir, to be dipped for your letters.

(*Bowing low.*)

I am a pen.

PEER GYNT (*bows lower still*)
Well, then I'm a leaf
Of imperial parchment come to grief.

HUSSEIN
My story, sir, I can put in one line:
They call me a blotter, but I'm a pen.

PEER GYNT
    And mine, Sir Pen, is quickly spun:
    I'm a blank sheet of paper, unwritten on.

HUSSEIN
    Nobody knows my true potential—
    They want me to soak up ink, that's all!

PEER GYNT
    For a woman, I was a silver-clasped book;
    Either mad or sane is a printer's mistake.

HUSSEIN
    Imagine—what a meaningless life—
    For a pen not to taste the edge of a knife!

PEER GYNT (*with a high leap*)
    Imagine—a reindeer, falling free—
    With never the hard earth under me!

HUSSEIN
    A knife! I'm blunt! See to my end!
    The world is chaos if I'm not sharpened!

PEER GYNT
    How sad for the world, when all that's self-made
    Was found by God Himself to be good.

BEGRIFFENFELDT
    Here's a knife!

HUSSEIN (*seizing it*)
                    Ah! To lap ink the better,
    What pleasure to cut oneself!

BEGRIFFENFELDT (*turning aside*)
                            Don't spatter.

PEER GYNT (*in mounting terror*)
    Hold him!

HUSSEIN
            Yes, hold me! Do what's proper!
    Hold! Hold the pen! Set me to paper!
                    (*Falls.*)
    I'm worn out. The postscript—fix it in mind:

He lived and he died in other men's hands!

PEER GYNT (*reeling*)
    What should I—! What am I? Oh Thou—take hold!
    I'm all that Thou willed—a Turk, a sinner,
    A hill troll—but help—somewhere it's failed—!

                (*Cries out.*)

    I can't remember your name—take hold,
    Thou—comfort of madmen, sustainer!

    (*Falls in a faint.* BEGRIFFENFELDT, *a wreath of straw
            in his hand, leaps to sit astride him.*)

BEGRIFFENFELDT
    Look at him, blustering in the filth—
    Out of himself—! Crown him there!

                (*Presses the wreath down on* PEER'S
                        head and shouts.)

    Hail, hail the Emperor of Self!

SCHAFMANN (*in the cage*)
    Es lebe hoch der grosse Peer!

ACT FIVE

SCENE ONE

On board a ship in the North Sea, off the Nor-
wegian coast. Sunset and a threatening sky. PEER
GYNT, *a rugged old man with grizzled hair and*
beard, stands on the poop. He is partly dressed as
a seaman, with pea jacket and high boots. His
clothes are rather worn; he himself is weather-
beaten, and his face appears harder. The CAPTAIN
and the helmsman are at the wheel. The crew is
forward. PEER *leans on the ship's rail and gazes*
toward land.

PEER GYNT
That's Hallingskarv in his winter coat,
Lording it there in the evening light.
And Jøkel,[61] his brother, next in line;
He still has his ice-green mantle on.
And there, how lovely! It's Folgefannen,[62]
Dressed like a maid in the whitest linen.
No cutting up, you old characters!

    Stand your ground, like the stone you are.

CAPTAIN (*calling forward*)
    Two hands to the wheel—and the lantern set!

PEER GYNT
    It's blowing up.

CAPTAIN

               Aye. Storm tonight.

PEER GYNT
    Can we see the Ronde hills from here?

CAPTAIN
    Not likely—they're out behind the glaciers.

PEER GYNT
    Or Blaahø? [63]

CAPTAIN

           No; but from up the rigging
    You can see on a clear day to Galhøpiggen. [64]

PEER GYNT
    Which way is Harteigen? [65]

CAPTAIN (*pointing*)

              Thereabouts.

PEER GYNT
    Ah, yes.

CAPTAIN

       You seem to know these parts.

PEER GYNT
    When I shipped out, it was down this coast;
    And the dregs, they say, leave the bottle last.

        (*Spits and gazes toward shore.*)

    Up in those blue ravines and notches
    And narrow valleys, dark as ditches—
    And below, along the open fjord—
    There's where the people's life is shared.

        (*Looks at the* CAPTAIN.)

Not many houses here.

CAPTAIN

Aye, when
They build, it's few and far between.[66]

PEER GYNT
Will we land by morning?

CAPTAIN

About that,
If it doesn't get too rough tonight.

PEER GYNT
It's threatening westward.

CAPTAIN

It is.

PEER GYNT

I hope
You'll remind me when we settle up—
I want to do a good turn for each
Of the crew——

CAPTAIN

Thanks!

PEER GYNT

It won't be much.
I've grubbed for gold and lost it all—
Fate and I, we've had a quarrel.
You know what I have in the safe below;
That's it—the rest was the devil's due.

CAPTAIN
It's more than enough to raise your stock
With the home folk.

PEER GYNT

I have no relatives.
No one waiting till the old boy arrives—
At least you miss the scene on the dock!

CAPTAIN
Here comes the storm.

PEER GYNT

So remember then—
If any man here is really pressed,
I won't be niggling on the cost——

CAPTAIN

That's fair. They're mostly short of means.
They all have wives and children home,
And the wages barely get them by—
But if they brought in some extra pay,
They'd praise that day for a good long time.

PEER GYNT

What's that? They have wives and families?
Are they married?

CAPTAIN

Married? Aye, the whole flock.
But the one who's hardest pressed is the cook;
There's always black famine at his house.

PEER GYNT

Married? With someone there to wait,
Who's glad when they come?

CAPTAIN

Aye, as the poor
Do things.

PEER GYNT

So one evening they appear—
What then?

CAPTAIN

Oh, I guess the wife'd set
Out a special treat——

PEER GYNT

A lamp on the table?

CAPTAIN

Maybe two—and a brandy, double.

PEER GYNT

And they sit, snug and warm by the fire—?
Children around them—the whole room astir—

And nobody's words are heard to the end
For the joy they feel——

CAPTAIN

                    You understand;
And that's why it's fair that you offered to fill
Their pockets a bit.

PEER GYNT (*pounds the railing*)
                    Damned if I will!
You think I'm mad? That I'll fork out
To take care of somebody else's brats?
I've slaved like a dog to make my mint!
No one's waiting for old Peer Gynt.

CAPTAIN

Do as you please; your money's your own.

PEER GYNT

Right! It's nobody else's but mine.
We'll settle as soon as the anchor's struck.
My cabin passage from Panama here;
A round of drinks for the crew. No more.
If I add a penny, you give me a smack!

CAPTAIN

You'll have my receipt, and not a brawl—
Excuse me; we're heading into a gale.

(*He crosses the deck forward. It has now grown
dark; lights are lit in the cabin. The sea runs higher.
                    Fog and thick clouds.*)

PEER GYNT

To leave a whole tribe of children behind—
To sow delight in their growing minds—
To be borne by others' thoughts on your way—!
There's no one ever who thinks of me—
A lamp on the table? I'll put it out.
Just let me think—! I'll get them tight—
Not one of the clods'll go sober ashore.
They'll break in drunk on those family groups!
They'll curse and hammer the table tops—
And stiffen their own with the breath of fear!

The wives'll scream and bolt from the house—
And the children too! Now let 'em rejoice!

(*The ship heels over; he staggers and holds
his balance with difficulty.*)

Well, that was a lively roll. The ocean
Works as if it were paid on commission.
It's still its old self by the northern skerries;
The riptide plotting its treacheries—

(*Listens.*)

What were those shouts?

THE WATCH (*forward*)

A wreck on the lee!

CAPTAIN (*amidships*)
Wheel hard starboard! Close to the wind!

THE MATE
Are there men aboard?

THE WATCH

I make out three!

PEER GYNT
Lower a boat——

CAPTAIN

She'd be swamped and drowned!

(*Goes forward.*)

PEER GYNT
Who thinks of that?

(*To several of the crew.*)

You'll try, if you're men!
What the hell if you wet your skins——

THE BOATSWAIN
It can't be done in a sea like this.

PEER GYNT
They're screaming again! And the wind is dying—

Cook, will you try? Quick! I'm paying——

THE COOK

For twenty pounds sterling, I'd refuse——

PEER GYNT

You curs! Cowards! Are you forgetting,
Those men have wives and children waiting
At home for them——

THE BOATSWAIN

　　　　　　Patience does wonders.

CAPTAIN

Bear off the breakers!

THE MATE

　　　　　　The wreck's gone under.

PEER GYNT

And in silence——

THE BOATSWAIN

　　　　　If they *were* married, right this minute
The world's got three fresh-baked widows in it.

(*The storm increases.* PEER GYNT *moves aft.*)

PEER GYNT

There's no faith left among men any more—
No Christian love, as it's written and taught—
Few good deeds, and still less prayer—
And no respect for the Deity's might.
In a storm like this, the Lord God rages.
Those beasts should remember, they take a chance,
That it's dangerous playing with elephants—
But instead, they're openly sacrilegious!
But *I* have no guilt, when I can prove
I was there with my money, ready to give.
And what do I get for it—? It's been said:
"A conscience at ease is a downy pillow." [67]
Oh yes, on land that can't be denied;
But on board ship, it isn't worth mud
To be honest among that rabble below.
At sea, you can't be yourself at all;

You follow the crowd from deck to keel.
Let judgment strike for the bo'sun or cook,
And I go plunging down with the pack—
Personal values don't have any place—
You rate like a hog in a slaughterhouse—
   It's my mistake that I've been too soft,
With nothing to show for it, only reproach.
If I were younger, my ways would shift
And I'd try playing the boss for a stretch.
There's time for it still! The parish'll hear
How Peer came swaggering home from afar!
I'll win back the farm by hook or crook,
Rebuild it, give it a regal look
Like a castle. Ah, but they can't come in!
They can stand at the gate, cap in hand,
Begging and pleading—*that* I don't mind;
But they won't get a penny of mine, not one—
If *I've* howled under the whips of Fate,
Trust me to find people I can beat——

(*A* STRANGE PASSENGER [68] *appears in the dark at*
PEER GYNT'S *side and greets him amiably.*)

THE PASSENGER
   Good evening!

PEER GYNT
                    Good evening! What—? Who are you?

THE PASSENGER
   Your servant—and fellow passenger.

PEER GYNT
   Odd? I thought I was all alone here.

THE PASSENGER
   A false impression. It's over now.

PEER GYNT
   But it's certainly strange that I see you tonight
   For the very first time——

THE PASSENGER
                    I don't go out days.

PEER GYNT
Have you been sick? You're white as a sheet——

THE PASSENGER
I'm thoroughly healthy, otherwise.

PEER GYNT
What a storm!

THE PASSENGER
                    Yes, what a blessing, man!

PEER GYNT
Blessing?

THE PASSENGER
              The waves are as big as houses.
It's simply mouth-watering! Ah, can
You imagine, on a night like this, the losses
In shipwrecks, and the men that go down!

PEER GYNT
My God!

THE PASSENGER
                Ever seen a man who's choked—
Or been hanged—or drowned?

PEER GYNT
                            Please! Have some tact!

THE PASSENGER
The corpses laugh. But that laughter stings;
And mostly they've bitten off their tongues.

PEER GYNT
Get away from me—!

THE PASSENGER
                    One question. Wait!
Suppose, for example, we rammed a reef
And sank in the dark——

PEER GYNT
                        Do you think we might?

THE PASSENGER
    I hardly know what answer to give.
    But suppose now I float, and you join the ocean——

PEER GYNT
    Oh, rubbish——

THE PASSENGER
              It's only a supposition.
    But when a man's got one foot in the grave,
    He mellows and hands out little favors——

PEER GYNT (*reaching in his pocket*)
    Ho, money!

THE PASSENGER
           No; I'd be satisfied if
    You'd make me a present of your cadaver—?

PEER GYNT
    Now this is too much!

THE PASSENGER
                Just the body, you know!
    It's important for my research——

PEER GYNT
                      Will you go!

THE PASSENGER
    But, my dear sir, think—how you'll benefit!
    You'll be opened up and brought to light.
    I'm investigating the source of dreams,
    But I'll also go into your joints and seams——

PEER GYNT
    Be off!

THE PASSENGER
          But, friend—a dripping stiff—!

PEER GYNT
    Blasphemer! You've aided the storm enough!
    It's madness! In all this wind and rain
    And roaring sea, with every sign
    Of something ghastly due for this ship—

You have to tempt it to hurry up!

THE PASSENGER
I see you're not in a mood for discussion;
But time may force another conclusion—

(*With a friendly nod.*)

We'll meet when you're sinking, if not before;
Perhaps you'll be in a better humor.

(*Goes into the cabin.*)

PEER GYNT
Dreary companions, these scientists!
Damned freethinkers—

(*To the* BOATSWAIN, *passing by.*)

A word, mine host!
That passenger? Who is that lunatic?

THE BOATSWAIN
There's nobody else but you coming back.

PEER GYNT
Nobody else? That's certainly queer.

(*To a* YOUNG SAILOR, *leaving the cabin.*)

Who just went inside?

THE SAILOR
The ship's dog, sir!

(*Passes on.*)

THE WATCH (*crying out*)
Land dead ahead!

PEER GYNT
My box! My trunk!
All baggage on deck!

THE BOATSWAIN
You want us to sink?
We're busy.

PEER GYNT
>   Captain! I meant it in fun!
>   But I swear now, yes, I'll help the cook—!

CAPTAIN
>   The jib has sprung!

THE MATE
>   The foresail's gone!

THE BOATSWAIN (*screaming from the bow*)
>   Breakers under us!

THE CAPTAIN
>   She's going to strike!

>   (*The ship grounds. Noise and confusion.*)

S C E N E   T W O

*Close to land, among surf and skerries. The ship
is sinking. Through the fog, glimpses of a boat with
two men. A heavy sea breaks over it; it overturns; a
shriek is heard, then silence. After a moment the
boat reappears, bottom up.* PEER GYNT *comes to
the surface nearby.*

PEER GYNT
>   Help! A boat! Help me! I'll die!
>   God have mercy—as the Scriptures say!

>   (*Clutches the keel.*)

THE COOK (*comes up on the other side*)
>   Lord! Oh, God! For my babies' sake—
>   Be merciful! To my rescue! Quick!

>   (*Clings to the keel.*)

PEER GYNT
>   Let go!

THE COOK
>   Lay off!

PEER GYNT

I'll smack you!

THE COOK

Try!

PEER GYNT
I'll smash you to pieces, wait and see!
Let go! She'll carry one; no more!

THE COOK
I know that! Swim for it!

PEER GYNT

You swim!

THE COOK

Sure!

(*They fight; one of the* COOK'S *hands is injured;
he hangs on tight with the other.*)

PEER GYNT
Let go that hand!

THE COOK

Spare me, please!
Think of my children, what they'll lose!

PEER GYNT
I'm more in need of life than you;
I haven't had children up till now.

THE COOK
Let go! You've lived, and I'm still young!

PEER GYNT
Hurry up, sink—you'll wreck this thing.

THE COOK
Have mercy! Swim it, in heaven's name!
You break no hearts if you don't get home—

(*He screams and slips under.*)

I'm drowning—!

PEER GYNT (*seizing him*)
                I've got you by the hair
Of your head; say a "Lord's Prayer"!

THE COOK
   I can't remember—it's turning black——

PEER GYNT
   Just the essentials! Say it, quick!

THE COOK
   Give us this day—!

PEER GYNT
              Oh, cook, come on;
Whatever you need, you'll have it soon.

THE COOK
   Give us this day——

PEER GYNT
             The same old song!
It's obvious you've been a cook too long——

           (*His hold loosens.*)

THE COOK (*sinking*)
   Give us this day our——

           (*Goes under.*)

PEER GYNT
              Amen, friend!
You were yourself, right to the end—

       (*Draws himself up on the keel.*)

Where there's life, there's always hope——

THE STRANGE PASSENGER (*takes hold of the boat*)
   Good morning!

PEER GYNT
         Ai!

THE PASSENGER
           I heard a whoop—
Funny I should be meeting you.

Well? Did my prophecy come true?

PEER GYNT
Let go! There's hardly room for one!

THE PASSENGER
I'll swim with my left leg and hang on
By my fingertips over this cleat
On the keel of the boat. How's that?
But, apropos your body——

PEER GYNT
Shh!

THE PASSENGER
The rest, of course, is dead as a duck——

PEER GYNT
Shut your mouth!

THE PASSENGER
Just as you wish.

(*Silence.*)

PEER GYNT
Well?

THE PASSENGER
I'm speechless.

PEER GYNT
Satan's tricks—
What now?

THE PASSENGER
I'm waiting.

PEER GYNT (*tearing his hair*)
I'll go mad!
Who are you?

THE PASSENGER (*with a nod*)
Friendly.

PEER GYNT
What, beside?

THE PASSENGER

    What do *you* think? Know any other who's
    Akin to me?

PEER GYNT

             The devil is—!

THE PASSENGER (*softly*)

    But is it his way to illuminate
    Life's dark journey by means of fright?

PEER GYNT

    Oh, indeed! I suppose it's your claim
    That a messenger of light has come?

THE PASSENGER

    Even *once* in a half year, can it be said
    You've been shaken to the roots by dread?

PEER GYNT

    Of course one's afraid when danger bristles.
    But all your words, they twist like weasels——

THE PASSENGER

    My friend, have you even *once* in your life
    Known the victory that dread can give?

PEER GYNT (*looking at him*)

    If you've come to open me a door
    It's stupid you didn't come before.
    This is absurd, to choose a time
    When the ocean's swallowing me like foam.

THE PASSENGER

    Would the victory be more likely, then,
    By the fireside in your drowsy den?

PEER GYNT

    Well—but your words were laughable.
    How could you think they'd stir my soul?

THE PASSENGER

    Where I come from they value smiles
    As high as all the pathetic styles.

PEER GYNT
Each to his own; the barber thrives
On what puts bishops into their graves.

THE PASSENGER
The souls in funeral urns don't try
On weekdays to dress for tragedy.

PEER GYNT
Be off, you monster! Get away!
I won't die! It's the land for me!

THE PASSENGER
You needn't worry in *that* respect—
No one dies half through the last act.

(*Glides away.*)

PEER GYNT
There, he got it out at last—
He was a tedious moralist.

S C E N E   T H R E E

*A churchyard high in the mountains. A funeral in
progress. The* PASTOR *and the mourners are just
singing the final verse of a hymn.* PEER GYNT *is
passing by on the road.*

PEER GYNT
Here's another who's gone our mortal way.
Thanks be to God, it isn't me.

(*Enters the churchyard.*)

THE PASTOR (*over the grave*)
Now, as the soul goes out to meet its doom
And leaves the dust here, hollow as a drum—
Now, dear friends, we must set a few things forth
About this dead man's pilgrimage on earth.
He wasn't rich, nor could you call him wise;
His voice lacked force; his bearing, manliness;

What thoughts he spoke were hesitant and tame;
He scarcely seemed the master of his home;
And when he entered church, he'd sidle in
As if he begged his place with other men.

    From Gudbrandsdal he came, over the wicked
Winding roads, as a boy; and he remained.
And you remember how, to the very end,
He always hid his right hand in his pocket.

    That hand thrust in his pocket is the thing
That, in one's memory, stands pre-eminent—
That and a certain diffidence, a shrinking
Look, that marked him everywhere he went.

    But, though his chosen path in life was lonely,
And he kept himself a stranger to our breed,
We all knew what he struggled so to hide—
The hand he covered had four fingers only—

    I well remember, many years ago,
A morning down at Lunde. Conscripts had
Been called; a war was on; all talk was stayed
On Norway's griefs and the fate of those we knew.

    I watched the drafting. At a table sat
A captain, flanked by sergeants, and the mayor.[69]
Boy after boy was summoned to their fire,
Measured, questioned, signed as a new recruit.
The room was full; and outside on the square,
Loud laughter rang from the young folk gathered there.

    Another name was called. We saw approach
One who was pale as snow on the glacier's edge.
They told him to step up; and as he neared,
We saw his right hand bandaged in a clout.
He gulped and swallowed hard; he groped for words,
And yet, despite their bidding, stood there mute.
Ah, yes, at last! With burning cheeks, in a voice
That failed at times, then caught up with his breath,
He mumbled of some accident, a scythe
That cut his finger right off at the base.

    Then suddenly the room was deathly still.
Glances were exchanged; men set their jaws;
They stoned the boy with silence in their eyes.
He felt the hailstorm, but saw nothing fall.
And then the captain rose and, pointing to

The door, spat and rapped out one word, "Go!"
    And so he went. On both sides men drew back
And made a kind of gantlet to be run.
He reached the door; and then his courage broke—
He fled—up and up the wooded slope
Past the rockslides, treacherous and steep.
He had his home high in the mountains then——
    Some six months later, he came here to us
With mother and betrothed and baby child.
He rented land beyond the ridge, a field
Toward Lomb where the tracts of waste land rise.
He married just as soon as possible.
He built a house; he fought the stubborn soil
And made it yield, his efforts bravely shown,
Between the rocks, in the sway of yellow grain.
In church he kept his right hand in his pocket—
But at home, I'd say his fingers, though but nine,
Grew calluses as sore as those with ten—
One spring the torrent struck his farm and took it.
    They got out with their skins. A ruined man,
He started in anew to clear the land;
And by that fall, the smoke rose up again
Over a farmhouse built on safer ground.
Safer? Yes, from flood—but not from glaciers.
Within two years, a snow-slide crushed his labors.
    And yet no avalanche could touch his spirit.
He dug, he raked, he swept, he carted trash—
Till he could see, as winter's first snow flurried,
His house raised up a third time, clean and fresh.
    Three sons he had, three clever, active boys;
Time came for school, which lay a long way off—
To reach the parish road, they'd have to squeeze
Down snow-banked ledges clinging to the cliffs.
What did he do? He let the eldest shift
As best he could; but where no man would walk,
He'd lead the boy, tied by a line, and lift
The others in his arms and on his back.
    So year by year he toiled, and they grew up.
Some help from them now seemed a decent hope.
In the New World, three wealthy businessmen
Forgot their father here and all he'd done.

Shortsighted, he was that. He had no eyes
For anything beyond his family's will.
He found as meaningless as sounding brass
Words that ought to ring in the heart like steel.
This land, the race, all the shining dreams,
Weighed less to him than mist on mountain streams.

Yet he was humble, humble as men come;
That day in Lunde stripped his conscience naked—
As certain as his cheeks that burned with shame
And those four fingers hiding in his pocket.

Lost to his country's laws? Yes, if you want.
But one true light above the law prevails,
As sure as over Glittertind's [70] white tent
The piling clouds build higher mountains still.
No patriot, this man. For church as well as state,
A barren tree. But up where the wasteland shelves,
In his family circle where he saw his lot,
There he was great, because he was himself.
His inborn note was steadfast as a star.
His life was music, like a muted bell.
So, peace be with you, silent warrior,
Who fought the peasant's little fight, and fell.

It's not our place to sift the heart and soul—
That's not for dust, but for the Judge of all—
Still I believe—and here it must be said:
This man stands now no cripple to his God!

(*The mourners scatter and depart.* PEER
GYNT *remains behind alone.*)

PEER GYNT

Now *that's* what I call Christianity!
Nothing unpleasant to jar the mind—
And the subject—being oneself to the end—
Brought out in the pastor's eulogy,
Has everything in it to recommend.

(*Looks down into the grave.*)

Was it him, I wonder, that boy who cut
Off his finger one day not far from my hut?
Who knows? If I didn't stand with my staff
By the edge of this kindred spirit's grave,

I could almost believe it was *me* that slept
And heard in dreams my character wept.
It's really a beautiful Christian trait,
This casting of retrospective thought
In charity over the days gone by.
I wouldn't mind facing my destiny
At the hands of this excellent parish priest.
Well, I have a while, undoubtedly,
Before I'm called as the gravedigger's guest—
And as Scripture says: "It's all for the best—"
And: "Sufficient unto the day, its evil—"
And: "Don't borrow to buy the sexton a shovel—"
Ah, the church is the true consoler. Up
Till now, I've really not given it credit—
But how good it is to hear restated,
From the highest and surest authorship:
"Whatever ye sow, ye shall also reap."
We should be ourselves, that's the key;
All for yourself and your own, I say.
If your luck runs out, at least there's honor
In having lived in a principled manner.
Now homewards! What if Fortune frowns,
And the road ahead is hard and tortuous—
Old Peer Gynt will go it alone
True to his nature: poor but virtuous.

(*Moves on.*)

SCENE FOUR

*A hillside with a dried-out river bed and, beside it,
a ruined mill. The ground is torn up; everything is
desolate. Higher upslope, a large farm, where an
auction is taking place. A noisy crowd has gathered;
many are drinking.* PEER GYNT *is seated on a rubbish
heap by the mill.*

PEER GYNT
    Forward or back, it's just as far;

Out or in, it's a narrow door.
Time corrodes, and the stream wears out.
Remember the Boyg—and go roundabout.

A MAN IN MOURNING
Now there's only the rubbish here.[71]

(*Catches sight of* PEER GYNT.)

And strangers too? God save you, sir!

PEER GYNT
And you! This crowd looks well amused.
A christening, or a wedding feast?

THE MAN IN MOURNING
A housewarming, I'd call it instead—
Except it's a bed of worms for the bride.

PEER GYNT
And the worms are fighting for rags and scraps.

THE MAN IN MOURNING
It's the end of the song; so there it stops.

PEER GYNT
They all end alike, all the songs;
They're old; I knew them when I was young.

A YOUTH OF TWENTY (*with a casting ladle*)
Look what I bought! An antique piece!
Peer Gynt poured silver buttons from this.

ANOTHER
See mine! Two cents for a money sack!

A THIRD
That's nothing! Five for a peddler's pack!

PEER GYNT
Peer Gynt? Who was he?

THE MAN IN MOURNING
                 I only know Death
Was his brother-in-law. And Aslak the smith.

A MAN IN GRAY
    You're forgetting me! Had too much beer?

THE MAN IN MOURNING
    You're forgetting Hegstad, a storehouse door!

THE MAN IN GRAY
    True; but when have you been so delicate?

THE MAN IN MOURNING
    See if she finds Death so easy to cheat——

THE MAN IN GRAY
    Come, brother! A drink, for brotherhood's sake!

THE MAN IN MOURNING
    Brotherhood, hell! You've had a crock——

THE MAN IN GRAY
    Nonsense! Our bloodlines don't run so faint;
    We're all brothers in old Peer Gynt.

            (*They go off together.*)

PEER GYNT (*softly*)
    One meets acquaintances.

A BOY (*calls after* THE MAN IN MOURNING)
                            My dead mother
    Will haunt you, Aslak, if you drink your meal.

PEER GYNT (*getting up*)
    What the farmers say doesn't hold altogether:
    "The deeper you dig, the better the smell."

A YOUTH (*with a bearskin*)
    The Dovre-cat, look! Ready to stuff.
    He routed the trolls on Christmas Eve.

A SECOND (*with reindeer horns*)
    Here's that marvelous buck whose fleece
    Carried Peer Gynt down Gendin ridge.

A THIRD (*with a hammer, calls to* THE MAN IN MOURNING)
    Hi, Aslak, you remember this sledge?
    Is that what you had when the devil cut loose?

A FOURTH (*empty-handed*)
>Mads Moen, here's the invisible cloak
>That Peer Gynt and Ingrid flew with, look!

PEER GYNT
>Some brandy, boys! I'm feeling old—
>Let's have a beggar's auction held!

A YOUTH
>What have you to sell?

PEER GYNT
>   I have a castle—
>It lies in the Ronde, tough as a thistle.

THE YOUTH
>I bid a button.

PEER GYNT
>   Make it a pint.
>To bid any less would gall a saint.

ANOTHER YOUTH
>He's fun, the old boy!

(*A crowd flocks around.*)

PEER GYNT
>   Grane, my horse—
>Who bids?

ONE OF THE CROWD
>   Where is he?

PEER GYNT
>   Far to the west!
>In the sunset, lads! He can fly as fast—
>As fast as Peer Gynt could lie for a purse.

VOICES
>What else do you have?

PEER GYNT
>   Both gold and dross!
>I bought them cheap; I'll sell at a loss.

A YOUTH
>Put up!

PEER GYNT
>>One dream of a silver-clasped book.
>That you can have for a buttonhook.

THE YOUTH
>To hell with dreams!

PEER GYNT
>>>My empire, then!
>I'll throw it among you; catch as you can!

THE YOUTH
>Does it bring a crown?

PEER GYNT
>>>Of the finest straw.
>It'll fit the first man that gives it a try.
>And wait, here's more! The Prophet's beard!
>A rotten egg! [72] A gray hair, snared
>From a madman! All for him who can show
>Me a sign in the hills saying, "This is the way!"

THE SHERIFF (*just arrived*)
>Run on like that, my man, and you'll
>Find your way takes you straight to jail.

PEER GYNT (*hat in hand*)
>Most likely. But, tell me, who was Peer Gynt?

THE SHERIFF
>What trash——

PEER GYNT
>>Please! Just some account—!

THE SHERIFF
>Oh, they say he was such a wild romancer——

PEER GYNT
>Romancer—?

THE SHERIFF
>>Yes, anything brave and fine

He could weave into something *he* must have done.
Excuse me—I have to be law-dispenser——

(*Goes.*)

PEER GYNT
And where's this amazing fellow now?

AN ELDERLY MAN
Shipped out, he did—and went askew
In some foreign land where he never belonged.
Been a good many years since he was hanged.

PEER GYNT
Hanged? I see! Well, I'm not surprised.
Old Peer Gynt was himself to the last.

(*Bows.*)

Good-by—and thanks for all your trouble!

(*Goes a few steps, then pauses.*)

You gay young blades and lovely ladies—
Could I repay you with a fable? [73]

SEVERAL VOICES
Yes, you know one?

PEER GYNT

I'm always ready—

(*Comes closer; a strange look passes over him.*)

In San Francisco, I once panned for gold.
The town had more acrobats than it could hold.
One played the fiddle, using his toes;
Another fandangoed down on his knees;
A third one, I heard, wrote verse that he read
While a hole was bored in the top of his head.
For the acrobat fair, the devil came west
To try out his luck with all the rest.
His talent was this: he'd come on big,
Uttering grunts like an actual pig.
He was quite unknown, but he had a style.
Suspense ran high; the house was full.

He strode out in a cape cut sweepingly.
Man muss sich drapieren, as the Germans say.
But under his cape—which nobody guessed—
He had a live pig stowed up by his chest.
And now the representation began—
The devil, he pinched, and the pig struck a tune.
The work took the form of a fantasy
Of life through a pig's eye, from *A* to *Z*—
Till the grand crescendo, a slaughterhouse squeal;
Then the artist bowed low, and the curtain fell.
The critics weighed and discussed the results,
Defined the merits and labeled the faults—
Some found the vocal development scant;
The death-cry, for others, was mere technique—
But all were agreed in this: *qua* grunt,
The performer had laid it on much too thick.
So the devil got it; he had no sense,
Not to take stock of his audience.

(*Bows and departs. An uneasy silence
settles over the crowd.*)

SCENE FIVE

The eve of Pentecost.[74] *Deep in the forest. At a
distance, in a clearing, a hut with reindeer antlers
over the door.* PEER GYNT, *on his hands and knees,
picking wild onions.*

PEER GYNT
Here's one point of view. I hope, not the last—
One tries all things and chooses the best.
That's what I've done—up from Caesar
And now almost down to Nebuchadnezzar.
So I did have to go through Bible history—
The old boy's back in his mother's custody.
"Of earth thou art born," [75] says Holy Writ—
The main thing in life is to fill your gut.
But fill it with onions? Much too coarse;

I'll have to be clever and set some snares.
Here's good brook water; I won't parch—
And among the wild beasts, I'll have no match.
When I come to die—as it has to be—
I'll crawl in under a windfallen tree;
Like a bear, I'll heap leaves over my tatters
And carve in the bark, in ample letters:
"Here lies Peer Gynt, a decent soul,
Emperor of all the animals—"
Emperor?

(*Laughs silently.*)

In a gypsy's dream dominion!
You're no emperor; you're an onion.
And I'm going to skin you, Peer, old top!
No blubbering now; you can't escape.

(*Starts peeling an onion layer by layer.*)

This outer layer, like a torn coat—
It's the shipwrecked man on the drifting boat.
Here's the passenger layer, thin as paint—
But the taste has a dash of the real Peer Gynt.
The prospector life was a run for the money;
The juice is gone—if it ever had any.
And now this rough-skinned layer—why,
That's the fur trader up at Hudson's Bay.
The next resembles a crown—no, thanks!
That we'll throw away—it's a jinx.
Here's the archaeologist, brief and brassy.
And here's the prophet, green and juicy.
He stinks, as the Scripture says, of lies,
Enough to bring tears to an honest man's eyes.
This layer that curls in softly together
Is the man of the world, living for pleasure.
The next looks sick. It has streaks of black—
Meaning priests—and slaves on the auction block.

(*Pulls off several layers at once.*)

These layers just go endlessly on!
Shouldn't it give up its kernel soon?

(Pulls the whole onion apart.)

God, but it doesn't! To the innermost filler,
It's nothing but layers—smaller and smaller—
Nature is witty!

(Throws the pieces away.)

To hell with brooding!
Go lost in thought, and you stumble for sure.
Well, I can make light of that foreboding,
Solidly planted on all fours here.

(Scratches his neck.)

How strange it is, this business—life,
As it's called! It has cards up its sleeve;
But try to play them, they disappear,
And you hold something else—or empty air.

*(He has approached close to the hut,
catches sight of it and starts.)*

That hut? On the moor—! Hm!

(Rubs his eyes.)

It's as though
This building is one that I used to know—
The reindeer horns under the gable—!
A mermaid, fish-shaped down from the navel—!
Lies! No mermaid—! Nails—slats—
Bars for shutting out goblin thoughts—!

SOLVEIG *(singing in the hut)*
Now the room's ready for Pentecost.
My dearest boy, in some far land—
　　Will you come at last?
　If your load seems enormous,
　　Rest for a while—
　　True to my promise,
　　I'll wait for you still.

PEER GYNT *(rises, hushed and deathly pale)*
One who remembered—and one who forgot.
One who squandered—and one who could wait—

Oh, life——! No second chance to play!
Oh, dread——! Here's where my empire lay!

(*Runs down the forest path.*)

SCENE SIX

*Night. A moor with fir trees burnt out by forest
fire. Charred tree trunks can be seen for miles
around. Here and there patches of mist clinging to
the earth.* PEER GYNT *comes running.*

PEER GYNT
Ashes, fog, and dust, wind-driven——
There's enough to build with here!
Stench and rottenness within;
Only a whited sepulcher.
Dreams, romances, stillborn visions
Laid the pyramid's foundations;
Up from these a stonework rose
With the stairways made of lies.
"Spurn the truth; nothing's sacred."
Fly that from the highest banner;
Let the trump of judgment clamor:
Petrus Gyntus Caesar fecit.

(*Listens.*)

What sound is that, like children weeping?
Weeping halfway into song——
And by my feet, threadballs creeping——!

(*Kicks at them.*)

Out of my way! You don't belong——!

THREADBALLS (*on the ground*)
We are thoughts;
You should have thought us——
Legs to walk on
You could have brought us!

PEER GYNT (*going round them*)
　　I brought life to *one,* in rags—
　　And it had twisted, bandy legs!

THREADBALLS
　　We should have soared
　　In a blending choir—
　　Instead we roll
　　Like threadballs here.

PEER GYNT (*stumbling*)
　　Threadballs! Drones, you mean—! Stop!
　　You want to trip your father up?

　　　　　　　(*Flees.*)

WITHERED LEAVES (*flying before the wind*)
　　We are watchwords
　　You should have spoken!
　　See, while you dozed,
　　We were stripped and broken.
　　The worm has eaten us
　　Down to the root;
　　We'll never spread out
　　To garland fruit.

PEER GYNT
　　You've lived in vain, is that your fear?
　　Lie still; you'll make a good manure.

A SIGHING IN THE AIR
　　We are songs
　　You should have sung!
　　A thousand times
　　You bit your tongue.
　　Deep in your heart
　　We waited for you—
　　You never called.
　　We're poison now!

PEER GYNT
　　Then poison yourselves, right at the source!
　　What time did I have to waste on verse?

(*Tries a shortcut.*)

DEWDROPS (*dripping from the branches*)
We are tears
That were never shed.
Barbed ice that wounds
We could have thawed.
Now the barb is fixed
In the marrowbone;
The wound is closed;
Our strength is gone.

PEER GYNT
Thanks—I wept in the Rondesval—
And still I got it in the tail!

BROKEN STRAW
We are deeds
That you should have done!
The strangler, Doubt,
Has struck us down.
In the crack of doom,
Then we'll arrive
And state your case—
Till you cry, "Enough!"

PEER GYNT
Filthy tricks! You can't believe
I ought to be blamed for what's *negative*? [76]

(*Hurries away.*)

AASE'S VOICE (*far off*)
Ai, what a driver!
Hoo, I'm upset
In the new-fallen snow—
I'm chilled and wet—
Peer, where's the castle?
You've turned the wrong way.
The devil misled you;
He's guided the sleigh!

PEER GYNT
It's time a poor fellow picks up and runs.

If I had to carry the devil's sins,
I'd soon be flat on the hill for sure—
One's own are heavy enough to bear.

(*Runs off.*)

SCENE SEVEN

Another part of the moor.

PEER GYNT (*singing*)
A sexton, a sexton! Where's the throng?
Open your bleating mouths and sing;
To rim your hats, a mourning band—
I've many dead to walk behind!

(*The* BUTTON-MOLDER, *with a box of tools and a
large casting ladle, comes from a side path.*)

THE BUTTON-MOLDER
Greetings, old man!

PEER GYNT

Good evening, friend!

BUTTON-MOLDER
You're in a hurry. Where are you bound?

PEER GYNT
A funeral.

BUTTON-MOLDER
Really? My eyesight's poor—
Excuse me—but is your name Peer?

PEER GYNT
I'm called Peer Gynt.

BUTTON-MOLDER
What a stroke of luck!
It's precisely Peer Gynt I've come to take.

PEER GYNT
To take? What for?

BUTTON-MOLDER

> That's an easy guess.
I'm a button-molder; you go in this.

PEER GYNT
Why should I go?

BUTTON-MOLDER

> To be melted down.

PEER GYNT
Melted—?

BUTTON-MOLDER

> The ladle's empty and clean.
Your grave is dug; your coffin's made;
The worms in your body'll be well fed—
But the Master has instructed me
To bring in your soul without delay.

PEER GYNT
You can't—! Like this? Without a warning—!

BUTTON-MOLDER
It's a well-known ancient custom, concerning
Wakes and christenings, to keep the banner
Day a secret from the guest of honor.

PEER GYNT
That's true. These thoughts—they bewilder
Me. Are you—?

BUTTON-MOLDER

> You heard. A button-molder.

PEER GYNT
I see! A pet child has many nicknames.
So, Peer, *that's* where you land, it seems.
But, listen, this is a rotten trick!
I know I deserve a better shake—
I'm not as bad as maybe you think—
I've done lots of good on earth; to be frank,
My offenses, at worst, have all been minor—
I could never be called a major sinner.

BUTTON-MOLDER
    But, my friend, that precisely is your offense.
    You aren't a sinner in the larger sense;
    That's why you're let off the fiery griddle
    And go, like the rest, in the casting ladle.

PEER GYNT
    Oh, ladle or pit—what do I care?
    Lager and bock are, both of them, beer.
    Behind me, Satan!

BUTTON-MOLDER
                    You're not so naïve
    As to think I trot on a cloven hoof?

PEER GYNT
    Cloven hoof or fox's claw—
    Pack out! And stay this side of the law!

BUTTON-MOLDER
    My friend, you're making a big mistake.
    We're both in a hurry; so for clarity's sake,
    I'll explain your case as quick as I can.
    As you said yourself, you're scarcely one
    Who's made a name for exceptional sinning—
    You barely break even——

PEER GYNT
                        Now you're beginning.
    To talk some sense——

BUTTON-MOLDER
                    Not so fast there—
    But to call you virtuous wouldn't be right——

PEER GYNT
    I never laid any claim to that.

BUTTON-MOLDER
    You're average then, just middling fair.
    A sinner in the old flamboyant style
    One meets with nowadays hardly at all.
    There's more to sin than making a mess;
    A sin calls for vigor and seriousness.

PEER GYNT
    That's true enough; you can't be a piker.
    You have to plunge in like the old berserkers.[77]

BUTTON-MOLDER
    But you, my friend, you took sin lightly.

PEER GYNT
    Like a splash of mud, friend, delicately.

BUTTON-MOLDER
    Now we're agreeing. The sulfur pit
    Is hardly for one who dabbles in dirt——

PEER GYNT
    And therefore, friend, I can go as I came?

BUTTON-MOLDER
    No, therefore, friend, it's melting time.

PEER GYNT
    What are these tricks you've hit upon
    Back here at home while I've been gone?

BUTTON-MOLDER
    The custom's as old as the world's creation;
    It follows the laws of conservation.
    You've worked at the craft—so you know how
    A casting often turns out with a flaw.
    Suppose, say, a button was missing a loop;
    What did you do?

PEER GYNT
                    I threw it out.

BUTTON-MOLDER
    Ah yes, Jon Gynt was a waster all right,
    As long as his wallet was well filled up.
    But the Master, you see, is thrifty, he is;
    And that's why he's grown so prosperous.
    He throws out nothing as unrepairable
    That still can be used for raw material.
    Now *you* were planned as a shining button
    On the vest of the world, but your loop gave way;
    So you'll have to go into the rubbish carton

And merge with the masses, as people say.

PEER GYNT

But you can't mean to melt me together now
With Tom, Dick, and Harry into something new?

BUTTON-MOLDER

Yes, so help me, it's just what I mean.
We've done it to others, time and again.
It's what they do with coins at the mint
When the image has worn away too faint.

PEER GYNT

But why be so wretched miserly!
My dear good friend, let me go free—
A loopless button, a worn-out coin—
What's that to your Master, so great a man!

BUTTON-MOLDER

Oh, as long as there's spirit in you, it'll
Lend you some value as casting metal.

PEER GYNT

No, I say! No! Tooth and nail,
I'll fight against it! I won't, that's all!

BUTTON-MOLDER

But what else? Use the brain you were given.
You're hardly buoyant enough for heaven——

PEER GYNT

I'm easily pleased. I don't aim so high—
But I won't give one jot of myself away.
Let the old-time judgment settle my life!
Send me a while to Him with the Hoof—
Say a hundred years, if it comes to that;
I know I could manage to bear it out—
The torture is moral, so it must be gentle;
At least it can hardly be monumental.
Transition, it's called, in some famous line—
And, as the fox said: [78] "You wait; there comes
A deliverance soon; you can burrow in
And hope in the meanwhile for better times."
But this other—simply to disappear

Like a mote in a stranger's blood, to forswear
Being Gynt for a ladle-existence, to melt——
It makes my innermost soul revolt!

BUTTON-MOLDER

But, my dear Peer, why all the fuss
Over a technical point like this?
Yourself is just what you've never been——
So what difference to you to get melted down?

PEER GYNT

I've never been——? That's a funny thought!
Peer Gynt's been somebody else, no doubt!
No, button-molder, you judge in the dark.
If you saw into me, right to the quick,
You'd discover then that I'm solid Peer,
And nothing but Peer, to the very core.

BUTTON-MOLDER

Impossible. Here in my orders, you're named.
See, where it's written: "Peer Gynt; to be claimed
For setting his life's definition at odds;
Consigned to the ladle as damaged goods."

PEER GYNT

What nonsense! It's some other person they mean.
Does it really say Peer? Not Rasmus or Jon?

BUTTON-MOLDER

I melted them down a long time back.
Come quietly now, and no more delays!

PEER GYNT

Damned if I will! Oh, that'd be nice
If you heard tomorrow you'd make a mistake.
Better be careful, my excellent man!
Think of the burden you're taking on——

BUTTON-MOLDER

I have it in writing——

PEER GYNT

                              Just a little while!

BUTTON-MOLDER

What would you do then?

PEER GYNT
>   Get some proof
That I've been myself all of my life—
Since you find the point so debatable.

BUTTON-MOLDER
Proof? Of what kind?

PEER GYNT
                           Statements sworn—
Witnesses——

BUTTON-MOLDER
            The Master, I fear, would decline.

PEER GYNT
He wouldn't! Well, sufficient unto the day—
My friend, permit me the loan of myself;
I'll come back soon. We're born only once;
And it's hard for creatures like us to dissolve.
Yes; you agree?

BUTTON-MOLDER
                  All right; one chance—
But at the next crossroads, there we'll see.

(PEER GYNT *runs off.*)

S C E N E   E I G H T

Farther along on the moor.

PEER GYNT (*running full tilt*)
Time is money, as the Gospel says.
If only I knew where the crossroad lies!
It could be far, or it could be near—
The earth's like a red-hot iron floor.
A witness! A witness! To find even one!
Not likely here, on this barren plain.
The world's botched up. It stuns your wits
That a man has to prove his obvious rights!

(*A bent* OLD MAN, *with a staff in his hand and a*
bag on his back, trudges in front of him.)

THE OLD MAN (*stopping*)
Good sir—something for a homeless man?

PEER GYNT
Sorry—but I'm clean out of funds.

THE OLD MAN
Prince Peer! Ah no; so we meet again—?

PEER GYNT
But who—?

THE OLD MAN
He's forgotten his Ronde friends?

PEER GYNT
But you can't be—?

THE OLD MAN
The Troll King, yes!

PEER GYNT
The Troll King? Really? The Troll King! Speak!

TROLL KING
Oh, but I'm miserably down on my luck—!

PEER GYNT
Ruined?

TROLL KING
Stripped to my very self.
A tramp on the highway, starved as a wolf.

PEER GYNT
Hurrah! Such witnesses don't grow on trees!

TROLL KING
But you too, Prince, you're gray as a squirrel.

PEER GYNT
Dear father-in-law, the years leave scars.
Oh, well; let's drop private affairs—
And please, above all, no family quarrels.

I was headstrong then——

TROLL KING

Yes; ah, yes—
The Prince was young. And the things youth does!
But my Lord was wise in leaving his bride;
She'd only have brought him shame and bother;
For later, she went completely bad——

PEER GYNT
She did!

TROLL KING

It's wretched, the life she's had.
Just think—she and Trond are living together.

PEER GYNT
Trond who?

TROLL KING

Of the Valfjeld.

PEER GYNT

Oh, yes, him!
The one I took those farm girls from.

TROLL KING
But my grandson's grown up fat and strong,
With strapping children all over the land—

PEER GYNT
Yes, my dear man, but we can't talk long—
There's something quite different on my mind—
I'm caught in a rather awkward spot
Where I need a character affidavit—
You'd help me greatly if you could give it.
I'll raise some change; we can down a shot——

TROLL KING
Oh, really; could I help the Prince?
Then maybe you'd give me a reference?

PEER GYNT
Gladly. It's just that I'm pinched for cash
And have to be careful more than I'd wish.

But now, here's the thing. You must recall
The night I courted your daughter well——

TROLL KING

Of course, your Highness!

PEER GYNT

　　　　　　　　No more titles!
All right. By force, you were going to drill
My eyes and adjust my vision a little
And turn me from Peer Gynt into a troll.
But what did I do? I put up a fight—
Swore I'd stand on my own two feet;
I gave up love and power and glory
Since being myself was more necessary.
I want you to swear to that in court——

TROLL KING

No, but I can't!

PEER GYNT

　　　　　What do you mean?

TROLL KING

You want me to play the liar's part?
Remember, you put our troll gear on,
And tasted the mead—?

PEER GYNT

　　　　　　　You set the trap;
But I never took the ultimate step.
And a man's made of just that kind of thing.
It's the closing verse that makes the song.

TROLL KING

But, Peer, it's closed quite differently.

PEER GYNT

What rot is that?

TROLL KING

　　　　　When you went away,
You'd cut our motto in your coat of arms.

PEER GYNT

Motto?

TROLL KING
> That shrewd and severing term.

PEER GYNT
What term?

TROLL KING
> The one that parts human life
From trolldom: Troll, to yourself be enough!

PEER GYNT (*recoils a step*)
Enough!

TROLL KING
> Since then you've worked to serve
Our realm with every straining nerve.

PEER GYNT
I! Peer Gynt!

TROLL KING (*weeping*)
> It's so ungrateful!
You've lived as a troll, secret, deceitful—
You used the word I taught you to win
Your place as a well-established man—
And now you come back to me and sneer
At the motto you ought to be thankful for.

PEER GYNT
Enough! A hill troll! An egoist!
It must be nonsense; I know it must!

TROLL KING (*pulls out a bundle of old newspapers*)
Aren't you aware that we read our papers?
Here, look; you can see it in black and red,
How the *Bloksberg Post* accords you all proper
Praise, and the *Heklefjeld Times* [79] has displayed
Your story from the day you went abroad—
Want to read them, Peer? I'll give you leave.
Here's an article, signed by "Stallion-hoof."
And another, "On Troll Nationalism."
The writer makes the point that a simple
And natural trollish enthusiasm
Is worth far more than horns and a tail.

"Our *enough*," he says, "gives the mark of the troll
To man"—and you're his conclusive example.

PEER GYNT

A hill troll? Me?

TROLL KING

It's perfectly clear.

PEER GYNT

I might just as well have stayed on here,
Snug in the Ronde mountains, right?
Spared toil and trouble and tired feet!
Peer Gynt—a troll? You lunatic, you!
Good-by! Here's something to buy tobacco.

TROLL KING

No, Prince!

PEER GYNT

Let go! You're out of your skull,
Or senile. Be off! Find a hospital!

TROLL KING

Ah, just the cure for my pains and aches.
But, as I told you, my grandson's brats
Have been taking over hereabouts;
And they're saying I only exist in books.
Your relatives always treat you worst:
I've heard that said, and I've learned it's true.
It's hard being only a legend now—

PEER GYNT

So many have been in that way cursed.

TROLL KING

And we trolls, we have no pension plans,
No mutual savings, or home relief—
In the Ronde they'd hardly be in line.

PEER GYNT

Thanks to that damned, "To yourself be enough"!

TROLL KING

Oh, the Prince doesn't have any cause for complaint.

And now, if somehow or other you could——

PEER GYNT

My man, you're sniffing on the wrong scent;
As it stands with me, I haven't a shred——

TROLL KING

Is it really true? His Highness, a beggar?

PEER GYNT

To the core. My princely ego spoils
In hock. It's your fault, you hellish trolls!
That shows what low company can augur.

TROLL KING

There goes another one of my hopes!
Farewell! It's not far to town, I'd judge——

PEER GYNT

What will you do there?

TROLL KING

                    Go on the stage.
The papers are calling for national types——

PEER GYNT

Good luck on your journey. Greet them from me.
If I can break loose, I'll go the same way.
I'll write them a farce, half gall, half candy,
And call it, *"Sic transit gloria mundi."*

> (*Runs off down the road, as the* TROLL KING
> *shouts after him.*)

SCENE   NINE

At a crossroads.

PEER GYNT

You're in for it, Peer—and then some!
The trolls' *enough* has sealed your doom.
The ship is wrecked. Cling to the spars!

What else? Melting could only be worse!

BUTTON-MOLDER (*at the parting of the ways*)
Well, where's your affidavit, Peer?

PEER GYNT
Is this the crossroads? Here, so soon?

BUTTON-MOLDER
I can read on your face, bold as a sign,
How the message goes; I've read it before.

PEER GYNT
I'm tired of running—it does no good——

BUTTON-MOLDER
Yes; and besides, where does it lead?

PEER GYNT
True. To a forest, in the dead of night ——

BUTTON-MOLDER
But there's an old tramp. Shall we have him wait?

PEER GYNT
No, let him go. He's been drinking, man!

BUTTON-MOLDER
But perhaps——

PEER GYNT
                    Shh; no—leave him alone!

BUTTON-MOLDER
Well, shall we start?

PEER GYNT
                    One question only.
What is it, "to be yourself," in truth?

BUTTON-MOLDER
A curious question out of the mouth
Of someone who recently——

PEER GYNT
                              Answer me plainly.

BUTTON-MOLDER

To be yourself is to slay yourself.[80]
But on you, that answer's sure to fail;
So let's say: to make your life evolve
From the Master's meaning to the last detail.

PEER GYNT

But suppose a man never gets to know
What the Master meant with him?

BUTTON-MOLDER

He has intuitions.

PEER GYNT

Intuitions can often be wrong and draw
A man *ad undas* in his profession.

BUTTON-MOLDER

Of course, Peer Gynt; but closing them out
Gives Him with the Hoof the choicest bait.

PEER GYNT

This thing is complicated at best—
All right; that I've been myself, I'll waive—
It's maybe too difficult to prove.
I'll accept that part of the case as lost.
But just now, walking the dew and drench,
I felt the shoes of my conscience pinch,
And I said to myself: yes, you have sins——

BUTTON-MOLDER

You're not going to start all over again——

PEER GYNT

No, not at all; great ones, I mean.
Not only in deeds, but thoughts and plans.
Abroad, I lived in dissipation——

BUTTON-MOLDER

Perhaps; but I have to see the list.

PEER GYNT

Well, give me time; I'll find a priest,
Confess, and bring you a declaration.

BUTTON-MOLDER

Yes, bring me that, and I can promise
You won't have the casting ladle to face.
But my orders, Peer——

PEER GYNT

That paper's old;
I'm sure it's already obsolete—
There was a time when my life was wild;
I played the prophet and trusted in Fate.
Well, may I try?

BUTTON-MOLDER

But—!

PEER GYNT

Come on now—
You can't have so very much to do.
Here in this district, the air's so sweet,
It makes the people age more slowly.
You know what the Justedal pastor [81] wrote:
"It's rare that anyone dies in this valley."

BUTTON-MOLDER

To the next crossroads; not a step beyond.

PEER GYNT

A priest, if he has to be tied and bound!

(*Runs off.*)

SCENE TEN

A hillside with heather, and a path winding over the ridge.

PEER GYNT

"This could be useful for many things,"
Said Esben, finding the magpie's wing. [82]
Who would have thought the sins I've done
Would save me when the night came on.
Well, as it is, it's a drastic cure,

To go from the frying pan into the fire—
Still there's an adage you can't escape—
Namely, that while there's life, there's hope.

(*A* LEAN PERSON, *dressed in a priest's cassock*
kilted up high and carrying a fowling net over his
shoulder, comes hurrying along the slope.)

Who's that? A priest with a fowling net!
Hi! I'm Fortune's child, all right!
Good evening, Pastor! This path is foul——

THE LEAN ONE
  It is; the things one does for a soul.

PEER GYNT
  Ah, someone's soon for heaven?

THE LEAN ONE

                                No;
  It's somewhere else I hope he's due.

PEER GYNT
  Could I walk with you, Pastor, a little way?

THE LEAN ONE
  With pleasure; I'm fond of company.

PEER GYNT
  I'm quite disturbed—

THE LEAN ONE

                Heraus! Explain!

PEER GYNT
  You see here before you a decent man.
  I've always obeyed our country's laws;
  Never been booked in a station house—
  But a man can sometimes lose his footing
  And stumble——

THE LEAN ONE

                It plagues the best of us.

PEER GYNT
  You know, small things——

THE LEAN ONE

            Just trifles?

PEER GYNT

                      Yes;
To me, sin *en gros* is nauseating.

THE LEAN ONE
Then, my dear man, find someone else;
I'm not what you seem to think I am—
You stare at my fingers? What of them?

PEER GYNT
You have such developed fingernails.

THE LEAN ONE
And now my feet? Do you disapprove?

PEER GYNT (*pointing*)
Is that hoof natural? [83]

THE LEAN ONE

            So I believe.

PEER GYNT (*raising his hat*)
I could have sworn that you were a priest;
And now I've the honor—— Well, all for the best.
When the front's door's open, skip the back way;
When the king appears, tell the help good-by.

THE LEAN ONE
Shake hands! You seem unprejudiced.
Well, friend, what can I do to assist?
Now please, don't ask for money or power;
I haven't got them to give any more.
It's shameful how business has fallen off;
There's not enough market to feed a dwarf—
Souls aren't moving; just now and again,
A stray——

PEER GYNT

        Has the race advanced so far?

THE LEAN ONE
On the contrary, it's slipping lower—

The majority end in a melting spoon.

PEER GYNT
Oh yes—I heard about that one time.
In fact, it's the reason why I've come.

THE LEAN ONE
Speak out!

PEER GYNT
        If it wouldn't be indiscreet,
I'd be so glad——

THE LEAN ONE
            For a lodging place?

PEER GYNT
You guessed what I need exactly, yes.
Business, you say, has suffered a lot;
So maybe you might relax a rule——

THE LEAN ONE
But, friend——

PEER GYNT
          My demands are very small.
A salary is hardly necessary;
Just kind treatment, if that's the story——

THE LEAN ONE
A heated room?

PEER GYNT
         Not overly warmed—
Mainly a chance to leave unharmed—
The right, as they say, to transfer out
If a better position comes to light.

THE LEAN ONE
This makes me truly sorry, friend—
But you can't imagine how many requests
Of a similar type I've heard expressed
By those departing their mortal round.

PEER GYNT
But when I think over my former life,

I know that I'm highly qualified——

THE LEAN ONE
They were only trifles——

PEER GYNT

                    That's what I said;
But now I remember, I traded in slaves——

THE LEAN ONE
There are men who've traded in minds and wills,
But done it badly, and lost their appeals.

PEER GYNT
I've packed out idols to the Orient.

THE LEAN ONE
Mere quibbles! Pure divertissement.
People pack idols of a viler sort
Into sermons, literature, and art—
And they stay outside——

PEER GYNT

                    But the worst of it
You couldn't guess—I played a prophet!

THE LEAN ONE
Abroad? Humbug! The end of most subtle
Sehen ins Blaue is the casting ladle.
If that's all you have to support your case,
With the best good will, I'll have to refuse.

PEER GYNT
But wait; in a shipwreck—I clung to a boat—
"Drowning men clutch at straws"—there's proof;
And, "It's every man for himself"—I quote—
Well, I halfway deprived a cook of his life.

THE LEAN ONE
I couldn't care if you'd half deprived
A kitchenmaid of what she saved.
What kind of stuff is this "halfway" talk?
Begging your pardon, but I wish you'd tell
Me who's going to waste expensive fuel,
In times like these, on such poppycock?

Now don't get mad; it's your sins I mean,
Not you; forgive me for speaking plain.
Listen, my friend, don't be absurd;
Prepare yourself for the melting spoon.
What would you gain by my bed and board?
Consider; you're a sensible man.
Well, you'd have memory, that's quite true—
But in the country of memory, the view
Would, both for your mind and heart, afford
"Mighty poor sport," as the Swedes complain.
You've nothing to groan or to smile about;
Nothing to fill you with joy or despair;
Nothing to make you run cold or hot; [84]
Only a secret, gnawing fear.

PEER GYNT

As they say: it isn't that easy to state
Where the shoe hurts when it's not on your foot.

THE LEAN ONE

That's true; I have—thanks to so-and-so—
No need for more than a single shoe.
But it's fortunate one of us brought up shoes;
It reminds me I have to be hurrying on—
I'm fetching a roast that's far from lean;
I can't stand around, shooting the breeze——

PEER GYNT

May I ask what fodder of sin you used
To fatten the man?

THE LEAN ONE

                    I was advised
That he'd been himself in every respect;
And that, after all, is the crucial fact.

PEER GYNT

Himself! Does *that* group belong to you?

THE LEAN ONE

It all depends. Some have gone through.
Remember, there are two ways that a man
Is himself; two sides, right and wrong, to a coat.
You know they've discovered in Paris of late,

How to make portraits by means of the sun.
The picture comes either direct and alive,
Or else in the form of a negative.
In the latter the lights and shadows reverse;
The casual eye will find it coarse—
But the likeness is there for all of that,
And it only remains to bring it out.
Now if, in the path of its life, a soul
Records itself in the negative way,
The plate doesn't go in the rubbish pile—
Rather, it's simply turned over to me.
I take it and treat it in suitable fashion
And gradually work a transformation.
I steam and I dip, I burn and rinse
With sulfur and other ingredients,
Till it has the image it ought to have—
Or as people call it, the positive.
But with someone like you that's half erased,
Sulfur and lye just go to waste.

PEER GYNT

So one has to come to you black as a crow
To become a white grouse? May I ask you now
The name of this negative counterfeit
That you're going to bring to the positive state?

THE LEAN ONE

The name's Peter Gynt.

PEER GYNT

                        Peter Gynt? Ah, yes!
Is he himself?

THE LEAN ONE

                He swears that he is.

PEER GYNT

Well, he can be trusted, this same Herr Peter.

THE LEAN ONE

You know him perhaps?

PEER GYNT

                        Oh, just a smatter—

One knows so many——

THE LEAN ONE

                I've got to skip;
Where last did you see him?

PEER GYNT

                  Down by the Cape.

THE LEAN ONE
Di buona speranza?

PEER GYNT

             Yes, but I'd guess
He'd be sailing soon, if I'm not amiss.

THE LEAN ONE
Then I'd better be heading down there quick.
If I only can catch him now in a hurry!
That Cape of Good Hope, it makes me sick—
It's been ruined by Stavanger [85] missionaries.

        (Rushes off southwards.)

PEER GYNT
The stupid dog! There he's racing off
With his tongue hanging out. That's a laugh.
What a pleasure it is to fool such an ass
With his precious airs and his solemn face!
He thinks he has something to swagger about!
His job isn't likely to make him fat—
He'll fall from his perch, with all that's his.
Hm! I'm hardly quite sure of my own—
Expelled, as it were, from the self-made men.

    (A falling star is seen. He nods after it.)

Here's from Peer Gynt, Brother Shooting-Star!
Shine, flash down, and disappear—

*(Pulls himself together apprehensively and goes
deeper into the mists; silence for a moment;
        then he cries:)*

Is there no one, no one to hear me even—
No one in darkness, no one in heaven—!

*(Re-emerges farther down, throws his hat on the
path and tears at his hair. Gradually a stillness
comes over him.)*

So unspeakably poor, then, a soul can go
Back to nothingness, in the misty gray.
You beautiful earth, don't be annoyed
That I've left no sign I walked your grass.
You beautiful sun, in vain you've shed
Your glorious light on an empty house.
There was no one within to cheer and warm—
The owner, they tell me, was never at home.
Beautiful sun and beautiful earth,
All you gave to my mother went to beg.
Nature is lavish; the spirit is mean.
How costly to pay your life for your birth!
I want to climb up on the highest crag
And see the sunrise once again
And stare myself blind at the promised land;
Then let me be covered by drifting snows;
Scratch on a rock, "Here No One lies."
And afterwards—then—! Ah, never mind.

CHURCHGOERS *(singing on the forest path)*
O blessed morn,
When the tongues of God
Struck the earth like flaming steel!
From the earth reborn
Now the sons of God
Raise songs to praise His will.

PEER GYNT *(shrinking in fright)*
Don't look! It's desert there inside—
I fear I was dead long before I died.

> *(Tries to creep into the bushes, but
> stumbles out onto the crossroads.)*

BUTTON-MOLDER
Good morning, Peer! Where's your list of sins?

PEER GYNT
Don't you think I've been turning stones
For all I'm worth?

BUTTON-MOLDER
                    You met no one here?

PEER GYNT
  Only a traveling photographer.

BUTTON-MOLDER
  Well, your time is up.

PEER GYNT
                    Everything's up.
  The owl smells a rat. He hoots in his sleep.

BUTTON-MOLDER
  That's the matin's bell——

PEER GYNT (*pointing*)
                    What's that shining?

BUTTON-MOLDER
  Just light in a hut.

PEER GYNT
                    That sound growing louder?

BUTTON-MOLDER
  Just a woman's song.

PEER GYNT
                    Yes, *there's* the meaning
  To all my sins.

BUTTON-MOLDER (*seizing him*)
                    Put your house in order! [86]

  (*They have come out of the wood and
        stand near the hut.*)

PEER GYNT
  Put my house in order? That's it! Go on!
  Get away! If your ladle were coffin-sized—
  It still couldn't hold both me and my list!

BUTTON-MOLDER
  To the third crossroads, Peer; but *then*—!

  (*Turns aside and goes.*)

PEER GYNT (*approaching the hut*)
Forward and back, it's just as far.
Out or in, it's a narrow door.

(*Stops.*)

No! Like an endless, wild lament,
It tells me: return, go in where you went.

(*Takes several steps, but stops again.*)

Roundabout, said the Boyg!

(*Hears singing in the hut.*)

No! This time
Straight through, no matter how steep the climb!

(*He runs toward the hut. At the same moment,*
SOLVEIG *appears in the doorway, dressed for church,*
with a psalmbook wrapped in a kerchief and a staff
in her hand. She stands there, erect and mild.
PEER GYNT *throws himself down on the threshold.*)

Lay judgment on a sinner's head!

SOLVEIG
It's him! It's him! Praise be to God!

(*Gropes toward him.*)

PEER GYNT
Cry out how sinfully I've gone astray!

SOLVEIG
You've sinned in nothing, my only boy!

(*Groping again and finding him.*)

BUTTON-MOLDER (*behind the hut*)
The list, Peer Gynt?

PEER GYNT
Cry out my wrongs!

SOLVEIG (*sitting down beside him*)
You've made my whole life a beautiful song.
Bless you now that you've come at last!

And bless our meeting this Pentecost!

PEER GYNT
So then I'm lost!

SOLVEIG
　　　　　　That's for One to settle.

PEER GYNT (*with a laugh*)
Lost! Unless you can solve a riddle!

SOLVEIG
Ask me.

PEER GYNT
　　　　Ask you? Yes! Tell me where
Peer Gynt has been this many a year?

SOLVEIG
Been?

PEER GYNT
　　　With his destiny on him, just
As first when he sprang from the mind of God!
Can you tell me that? If not, I'm afraid
I'll go down forever in the land of mist.[87]

SOLVEIG (*smiling*)
O that riddle's easy.

PEER GYNT
　　　　　　What chance can you give!
Where have I been myself, whole and true?
Where have I been, with God's mark on my brow?

SOLVEIG
In my faith, in my hope, and in my love.

PEER GYNT (*starting back*)
What are you saying—? Don't play with words!
You're mother even to the boy inside?

SOLVEIG
I am, yes—but who is his father?
It's He who hears the prayers of the mother.

PEER GYNT (*a light breaks over him; he cries out:*)
  My mother; my wife! You innocent woman—!
  O, hide me, hide me within! [88]

(*Clings to her, covering his face in her lap.
  A long silence. The sun rises.*) [89]

SOLVEIG (*singing softly*)
  Sleep, my dear, my dearest boy,
  Here in my arms! I'll watch over thee——

  The boy has sat on his mother's lap.
  In play, they've used their life's day up.

  The boy's been safe at his mother's breast
  His whole life's day. May his life be blessed!

  The boy has lain so near to my heart
  His whole life's day. Now he's tired out.

  Sleep, my dear, my dearest boy,
  Here in my arms! I'll watch over thee!

BUTTON-MOLDER'S VOICE (*from behind the hut*)
  We'll meet at the final crossroads, Peer;
  And *then* we'll see—— I won't say more.

SOLVEIG (*her voice rising in the early light*)
  Sleep in my arms; I'll watch over thee—
  Sleep and dream, my dearest boy!

NOTES

Anyone attempting to pin down the diverse allusions of Ibsen's dramatic poem in a set of notes must necessarily be greatly indebted to Henri Logeman's *A Commentary on Henrik Ibsen's "Peer Gynt."* In addition to this acknowledgement, I would like to thank Professor Gunnar Høst and his wife Else Høst, as well as Professor Daniel Haakonsen, of the University of Oslo, for their help in resolving certain references familiar only to native-born Norwegians.

With proper names and place names, I have followed as far as possible the spellings of Ibsen's nineteenth-century Dano-Norwegian, rather than the later revisions of the language reformers he so cordially detested. In a few cases I have made or kept transliterations where euphony in English or precedents of usage seemed to recommend them: Boyg, for instance, for Bøyg in the original.

For a number of other instances, in which the original forms have been retained, some guide to Norwegian pronunciation might be useful. The *aa* diphthong is sounded like the *aw* in "flaw"; and the final *e* is pronounced: thus *Aase* is "AW-suh." The *ee* diphthong has the *ai* sound in "chair"; and *y* is equivalent to German *ü*: thus *Peer Gynt* is "PAIR GÜNT." The *a* has its full sound as in "fall"; and *j* is pronounced as *y*: thus *Valfjeld* is "VOL-f(yell)d." *Ei* has the sound of *ay* in "play"; final *g* is mute: thus *Solveig* is "SOL-vay." Among the vowels, *i* is pronounced *ee* (*Kari*, "KOR-ee"), and *ø* has the sound of German *ö*. As in Danish, the letter *d* within a word is often not pronounced: *Mads Moen* is "MAHSS MOAN." The above are only approximations, but they should allow an actor or reader to find intonations that have some flavor of the original.

1. *Gendin ridge:* A mountain edge between Lake Bygdin and Lake Gjendin in Jotunheimen, Norway.

2. *Where are the snows of yesteryear:* This expression, though originating in Villon's *"Où sont les neiges d'antan?"* had become assimilated in Norwegian and Danish.

3. *loafing in the chimney-corner home:* The hero of Norse fairy tales from at least as far back as the Middle Ages is the Askeladd, the male counterpart of Cinderella. Usually the youngest of three brothers, he holds the most menial position in the household and is assumed to be lazy, stupid, and incompetent. When he escapes from the narrow and humiliating conditions at home, however, he proves that, without difficulty, he can master any task set before him. He vanquishes trolls, confounds the king, and wins the princess and half the kingdom. Aase's denunciation is in part her hope that Peer will live out the Askeladd's destiny.

4. *Lunde:* A common name for a farm throughout Norway; so probably a large farm, consisting of as many as twenty-five to thirty buildings, virtually on the scale of a small village.

5. *changeling:* An ugly, malformed, or imbecilic child, thought to be the progeny of gnomes or evil spirits and substituted by them for a normal human child. One way that the mother could recover her own was to beat the changeling soundly, whereupon it would vanish through the air and the true child would reappear in the cradle.

6. *Engelland:* An old form, found in ballads and nursery rhymes, for England. Logeman observes that the name connotes the country of angels (Engel-land), suggesting that it must be taken as a vague, cloud-borne realm of chivalry and high romance.

7. *the halling:* The most acrobatic of the Norwegian folk dances, performed only by men, who dance alone, frequently to show off their agility before a girl.

8. *The Chief Cook:* The chief, or master, cook has a role

something like a master of ceremonies at a country wedding feast.

9. *It's high to this ceiling:* In the halling, it is considered a great feat for the dancer to kick the rafters. Here, in the open air, the young man is saying, his leaps will be even more spectacular.

10. *Hedal:* There is a Hedal near the Sprillen lake in Valdres and one in Gudbrandsdal. But as Solveig's parents come "from the west country," the former is the more likely reference.

11. *her prayer book wrapped in a napkin:* Peasant women had the custom, when going to church, of carrying their hymnbooks wrapped in their kerchiefs. Solveig's parents thus show their expectation that the wedding will be a solemn and religious one.

12. *I'm just confirmed:* About fifteen or sixteen years old.

13. *The soul of piety:* Solveig's father belongs to a sect of pietists, possibly that begun in the early nineteenth century by H. N. Hauge, whose followers were known as "the awakened ones"; therefore he would regard most forms of pleasure as sinful and to be avoided.

14. *Three Farm Girls:* Literally, three *seter* girls, the *seter* being the alpine meadows where the cattle were driven to pasture for the summer months, watched over by dairy maids, who lived an isolated life in the outfarms, or *seter*-huts.

15. *a three-headed troll:* Trolls came not only in the two- and three-headed varieties, but also with four, five, six, eight, nine, and twelve heads. But these hardly bore comparison with the Devil's grandmother, who, according to report, had three hundred.

16. *We won't have a bed lying empty now:* "Now," in the original, reads "this Saturday night." On Saturday evening, when the week's farmwork was done, the unmarried girls would retire, usually to the *stabur* or storehouse, and the young men would meet them in bed, although decorum dic-

tated that the strict rules of bundling must be observed. This was often the only way for young people to get to know one another, since it was considered effeminate for a young man openly to seek a girl's company.

17. *The Ronde Mountains:* A mountain group on the southeastern edge of the Dovre range.

18. *A Woman in Green:* Cf. Asbjørnsen, "Reindeer Hunt at Ronde," in which a hunter named Klomsrud falls in with fourteen green-clad women, green because they belong to the race of the *underjordiske*, those who live under the green sod and are thought to incorporate the souls of the dead.

19. *drawing his finger across his throat:* Probably with the implication of Polonius (*Hamlet*, II, 2), who points to his head and shoulders, saying, "Take this from this, if this be otherwise."

20. *The Royal Hall of the King of the Dovre Mountains:* Much of the basic material for this scene has been freely adapted from H. C. Andersen's charming tale, "Elf Hill" ("Elverhøj").

21. *to yourself be—enough:* Herman Weigand finds the conceptual equivalent of this phrase in Augustine's *De Civitate Dei*, Bk. XIV, Ch. 13. In discussing the fall of man, Augustine states that man's fundamental sin consists in "*sibi sufficere*," i.e., falling away from God, the source of all being. "*Sibi sufficere*," Weigand suggests, may have filtered down to the theological language of Ibsen's time in sermons or the catechism, to be exactly rendered, then, in the phrasing of the troll's motto.

22. *Our simple, domestic way of life:* "Under the figure of the trolls, the party in Norway which demands commercial isolation and monopoly for home products is most acutely satirized." Edmund Gosse, *Northern Studies*.

23. *food and drink:* The act of eating or joining with others in a common meal has a sacramental and binding character in many myths and rituals, e.g., the seven

pomegranate seeds that condemned Persephone to three months each year in the Underworld.

24. *our tails:* Trolls are most easily recognized by their tails, which link them both to prehuman existence and to the family and domain of Satan. The outward symbol of certain inward traits, the tail falls off of itself when the *huldre* (literally, one of the "hidden people," related to *hul*, hole, abyss, void), through marriage with a human being, is consecrated by the priest.

25. *Blackfrock's cows:* A reference to the cassock of the priest. The trolls identify the church bells, which they cannot abide, with cow bells.

26. *The Great Boyg:* The enigma of this symbolic presence has called forth a wide spectrum of interpretations. In Asbjørnsen's original folk tale, it is an invisible, apparently enormous troll. The word *bøyg* is related to the German *beugen*: to curve, meander, bend. Thus, some have identified the Boyg with the Midgardsorm of the Eddas, the world serpent coiled, like Okeanos, about the earth. Others have suggested that this voice speaking out of the darkness may be taken to be a voice out of the depth of Peer's own being. Groddeck describes it as "the self, the objective self, the opposite to the ego." On this point, as with everything else in the poem, the reader had best follow the Button-molder's advice and subordinate the commentators to what, intuitively, he feels is meaningful to him.

27. *the wingbeats of great birds:* Probably the sound of witches in flight, cf. Asbjørnsen, "Tales of a Sexton." Or possibly, the spirits of the dead, which also are often reincarnated in birds (cf. *New Golden Bough*, II: "Taboo and the Perils of the Soul," 151, and Add. Note). When the saga hero Sigurd killed the dragon Fafnir and tasted his heart's blood, he acquired a knowledge of the language of birds. But Peer, already partly in the trolls' power, by closing out the hero's mission he was born for, makes the birds his enemies.

28. *Soria-Moria Castle:* The name "Soria-Moria" comes from the Arabic and refers to a group of small islands out-

side the Red Sea which the Arabs believe to be the Isles of the Blessed.

29. *Grane:* The legendary horse belonging to Sigurd Fafnirbane.

30. *Mr. Cotton:* In his poem "Abraham Lincoln's Death" Ibsen designates John Bull as "the cotton magnate." And elsewhere, in a piece of drama criticism, he comments on "a complete Englishman, who is willing enough to help his friend, but by no means loses sight of cotton interests."

31. *Eberkopf:* Literally, "boar's head," an image suggesting recent Prussian aggressions.

32. *Trumpeterstraale: Literally,* "trumpet blast," a barbed thrust at Swedish nonintervention in the Prusso-Danish War.

33. *world-historical-fellowship:* In the original, *verden-borgerdomsforpagtning*—a nonsensical burlesque of German agglutinated words.

34. *if you won the earth entire and lost your self:* Cf. *Luke* 9:25; *Matthew* 16:26; *Mark* 8:36.

35. *Lippe-Detmold:* A small Westphalian principality, later incorporated in 1870 in the German Empire.

36. *Charles the Twelfth:* The Swedish warrior-king (1682–1718) who led campaigns against Denmark, Norway, Poland, Russia, and Turkey.

37. *Bender:* The town in which Charles XII is said to have torn the caftan of the Turkish vizier with his spurs for betraying his ambitions by concluding a truce with Russia.

38. *Goddam:* Ibsen inserts this old form of the oath, in English, in his Norwegian text. As far back as the fifteenth century, Joan of Arc had called the English soldiers in France "the Goddams" for their effusive swearing.

39. *Castalia:* Not a stream, but the celebrated fountain sacred in antiquity to Apollo and the Muses. It is situated on

Mount Parnassus, not Olympus, as Cotton seems to believe.

40. *Morning and evening are not alike:* Probably an allusion to *Psalms* 90:6, although there is also a recall of the Troll King's words in Act Two.

41. *Bus and I, why, we're relatives:* Darwin's theories had been introduced into Norway by way of thorough and intelligent expositions appearing in the magazine *Budstikken* for February and March, 1861.

42. *Bornu:* A region in the Sudan, south of the desert.

43. *Habes:* Or Habesch, the Arabic word for Abyssinia.

44. *Gyntiana:* In 1852, Ole Bull, the celebrated violinist, had founded a Norwegian colony in America, modeled after those of the French socialists, which he named "Oleana." The name and the fantastic claims advanced by the founder—here echoed by Peer—survive today in the well-known folk song.

45. *The ass in the ark:* Probably alludes to a venerable conundrum: Q. What ass brayed so loud that everyone in the world could hear it? A. The ass on Noah's ark.

46. *My kingdom . . . for a horse:* Cf. *Richard III*, V, 4.

47. *Ab esse ad posse:* The axiom in logic, *ab esse ad posse valet, ab posse ad esse non valet consequentia.* It is permissible to argue from fact to possibility, but not the reverse.

48. *Kaaba:* A small, cubical building in the court of the Great Mosque in Mecca, which contains the famous Black Stone, believed to have been given the prophet Abraham by the angel Gabriel.

49. *What did I ever want in that crew:* Cf. Molière, *Les Fourberies de Scapin*, II, 11, *"Que diable allait-il faire dans cette galère?"* This expression, too, had been absorbed in Norwegian.

50. *Das Ewig-Weibliche zieht uns an:* An intentional misquotation of the concluding lines of *Faust*: *"Das Ewig-Weibliche zieht uns hinan."* Goethe's "The Eternal Feminine draws us upward," filtered through the Gyntian soul, becomes "The Eternal Feminine lures us on."

51. *do you know what it is to live:* Peer's reply to his rhetorical question should be compared with Ibsen's own answer, phrased in a famous quatrain:

> What is life—but to fight
> In heart and mind with trolls?
> And poetry? That's to write
> The last judgment of our souls.

52. *Becker:* K. F. Becker's *Weltgeschichte,* published 1801–1809, and translated into Danish toward the mid-nineteenth century.

53. *The statue of Memnon:* Memnon was the son of the dawn, king of the Ethiopians, and lived in the extreme east, on the shore of Ocean. He and his warriors fought for Troy, where he was slain by Achilles. On his death, his mother Eos (Dawn) begged Zeus to grant him honor and immortality. Zeus did so by turning the sparks of his funeral pyre into birds, which rose, divided in two flocks, and fought until they fell back into ashes. Every year the battle of these birds, called Memnonides, is re-enacted. The enormous stone seated figure by the Nile at Thebes is said to give forth a sound like the breaking of a lyre string each morning at sunrise, which supposedly is Memnon greeting Eos. Ovid relates the story in Book 13 of the *Metamorphoses.*

The owl of wisdom was the emblem of the University of Christiania; so that, in the midst of Peer's historical phase, in a land burdened by a dead past, Ibsen would seem to be accusing the academics in his own country of doting on the dead past, rather than perpetuating and renewing their culture through song (poetry) and struggle (healthy controversy).

54. *Music . . . of the past:* An allusion to the *Zukunftsmusik* of Richard Wagner, whose book, *The Art Work of the Future,* had appeared in 1849.

55. *threescore and ten Interpreters:* The authors of the Greek version of the New Testament known as the Septuagint. No satisfactory explanation has been offered for the 160 more.

56. *my countryman Munchausen's fox:* Cf. Ch. 2, *The Adventures of Baron Munchausen.* The Baron, out hunting in a Russian forest, encounters a black fox whose skin is too fine to spoil by gunshot. He skewers the fox's tail to a tree with a spike nail, crosscuts his face with his hunting knife, and flogs him with his whip till he leaps out of his skin.

57. *Huhu:* A caricature of the *Maalstraevere,* the ultra-nationalist group of language reformers. As a result of Ivar Aasen's discovery in 1849 of the continuity of local Norwegian dialects with old Norse, and led by him and A. O. Vigne, the *maalstraevere* faction agitated against Dano-Norwegian in favor of return to the old language, renamed "New Norwegian" to give it an aura of modernity. *Foreign sirens* refers to the cultural domination of the Danes, who had ruled the country from the end of the fourteenth to the beginning of the nineteenth centuries. The orangoutangs are the Norse vikings, whose "growls and grunts" must be fostered in the peasant Malabaris.

58. *a Fellah carrying a mummy on his back:* A satire on the cult of the heroic Charles XII among the Swedes, who had proved themselves like their venerated "royal mummy," during the events of 1864, only in the lifelessness of their responses.

Of more general importance here is the fact that Ibsen is showing two forms of the self-preoccupied withdrawal from and distortion of reality that arises out of living in and for an irrecoverable past, first as it affects words, then as it affects deeds.

59. *In the likeness of a bull:* The sacred bull worshiped in Ptolemaic times as the earthly incarnation of the Egyptian god of the Underworld, Serapis (Osiris-Apis).

60. *Hussein, a government minister:* An allusion to the Swedish Foreign Secretary, Count Manderström, who had

thought to deter Prussian aggression with a flurry of diplomatic notes. F. L. Lucas aptly compares him to Neville Chamberlain.

61. *Hallingskary, Jøkel:* Mountains in the Hardanger district, along which the ship is coasting.

62. *Folgefannen:* An immense glacier between the Hardanger Fjord and its branch, the Sør Fjord.

63. *Blaahø:* Literally, in Norwegian dialect, "blacktop," the name of several peaks in Jotunheim.

64. *Galhøpiggen:* The highest mountain (8097 ft.) in Scandinavia, near the end of the Sogne Fjord in Jotunheim.

65. *Harteigen:* A mountain east of Odda in Hardanger.

66. *when they build it's few and far between:* In 1886, Ibsen wrote to a German friend: ". . . he who would know me fully must know Norway. The grand but austere nature with which people are surrounded in the North, the lonely, isolated life—their homes often lie many miles apart—compel them to be indifferent to other people and to care only about their own concerns; therefore they become ruminative and serious-minded; they ponder and doubt; and they often despair. With us every other man is a philosopher. Then there are the long dark winters, with the thick fog about the houses—oh, they long for the sun!"

67. *A conscience at ease is a downy pillow:* Peer probably is thinking of the German proverb: *Ein gutes Gewissen ist ein sanftes Ruhekissen.*

68. *The Strange Passenger:* This personification of Peer's destiny as guide has been variously interpreted—as Peer's double, as an emissary from the supernatural world, or as a projection of Kierkegaardian dread.

69. *mayor:* I.e., *lensman,* rural mayor (Brynildsen, *Norsk-Engelsk Ordbok*), that is, the chief civil authority in a district. The titles of functionaries, being intrinsically bound up

with the particular social system of a country, are the translator's despair.

70. *Glittertind:* A peak almost as high as its close neighbor, Galhøpiggen. Its summit is covered by a snow mantle nearly one hundred feet thick.

71. *Now there's only the rubbish here:* In this scene, relationships that have developed during Peer's long absence are made to surface and disappear in such obscurity that some explanation seems called for. Both Hegstad and Ingrid have apparently gone decidedly downhill since Peer's bride-rape. Aslak (The Man in Mourning) has married her; he shows, however, no great love for her, perhaps because her ways have become too free and easy even for him, though Mads Moen (The Man in Gray) observes that Aslak has never been overly delicate. Their conversation degenerates into a coarse joke that Ingrid may yet cheat Death: i.e., Death has been the last of her several lovers. Considering the time lapse, the boy is hardly Peer's child, as some have conjectured, but Aslak's or, perhaps, Mads Moen's.

72. *A rotten egg:* In the original, a wind egg, i.e., one which has lost power of development and become putrid.

73. *a fable:* Peer's adventure in San Francisco is adapted directly out of Phaedrus, *Fabulae*, V, 5, "Scurra et Rusticus." In the original fable, after the buffoon has won the prize for the realism of his grunts, the countryman produces the real pig from under his cloak, rebuking his audience with the words: "Look, this shows what sort of judges you are."

74. *The eve of Pentecost:* In the north of Europe, the later feast of Pentecost, rather than Easter, is the time chosen for the baptism of adults. The ceremony of the descent of the Spirit, however, is central to the emphases Ibsen wishes to develop, as against the more familiar Easter symbolism in such works as *The Divine Comedy* and *Faust*.

75. *Of earth thou art born:* Cf. *Genesis* 3: 19 (or *Eccles.* 12:7), characteristically misquoted by Peer.

76. *What's negative:* A play upon Hegelian terminology,

in which "the negative"—that which opposes the primary thesis—is responsible in turn for the higher concept, the synthesis.

77. *the old berserkers:* A class of legendary warriors who, in battle, fought in a frenzied rage, howled, bit their shields, foamed at the mouth, and were generally thought invulnerable. Peer briefly imitates their spirit in the Boyg scene when he bites his own arm.

78. *as the fox said:* A reference to the proverb: "This is a change," said the fox as they flayed him.

79. *Bloksberg . . . Heklefjeld:* The Blocksberg, where German as well as Norwegian witches gathered for their great sabbaths on the Eve of May Day (Walpurgis Night) and Midsummer Eve, is commonly identified with the Brocken, the highest peak of the Harz Mountains. The Hekla Mountain in Iceland is another similar trysting place.

80. *To be yourself is to slay yourself:* This prescription has overtones of *Matthew* 16: 25–26, but more directly concerns the choice first stated and now recently revived by the Troll King, namely, to kill one's self-sufficiency in order to become the open, full, and true self. The nature of the latter is eloquently indicated by Ibsen's French translator, Count Prozor, as follows: *"Être soi-même, ce n'est pas être Peer Gynt ou un autre, c'est être homme, c'est tuer en soi ce que Peer appelle orgueilleusement le moi Gyntien pour y faire vivre le moi humain."*

81. *the Justedal pastor:* Matthias Foss (1714–1792) became the parish priest of Justedal in 1742 and, eight years later, wrote a "short description of Justedal" in which this claim is advanced.

82. *Esben, finding the magpie's wing:* Refers to the folk tale "The Princess That No One Could Silence," in which Esben Askeladd finds a cringle, then a potsherd, and finally a dead magpie, and these apparently worthless things enable him to win "the princess and half the kingdom."

83. *Is that hoof natural:* The Devil in Norwegian folk-lore is represented as having a single hoof.

84. *Nothing to make you run cold or hot:* Cf. *Revelation* 3: 15–16.

85. *Stavanger:* The Norwegian Missionary Society, founded in 1842, had its headquarters in Stavanger.

86. *Put your house in order:* Cf. *Isaiah* 38:1.

87. *the land of mist:* According to the Eddas, there was once no heaven above nor earth beneath, but only a bottomless deep, and a world of mist in which flowed a fountain that froze into rivers of ice. The world of mist was contrasted with the world of light lying to the south.

88. *hide me within:* Cf. *John* 3:3–7.

89. *The sun rises:* In the folk tales, the troll monster can only remain abroad until dawn, whereupon this primeval mountain spirit is changed back ("stone thou wast, to stone returnest") into its element, symbolically vanquished, as when the first rays of the Light of the World were shed on it.

SIGNET CLASSICS from Around the World

THE STORY OF GOSTA BERLING *by Selma Lagerlöf*
  An unfrocked minister's picaresque search for redemption
  amidst the farmlands and folk of 19th century Sweden. A
  new translation with an Afterword by Robert Bly.
  (#CT125—75¢)

THE BROTHERS KARAMOZOV *by Fyodor Dostoyevsky*
  Complete and unabridged, the great classic about a passion-
  ate and tragic Russian family. Translated by Constance
  Garnett. Revised, with a Foreword by Manuel Komroff.
  (#CT33—75¢)

NOTES FROM UNDERGROUND, WHITE NIGHTS, THE DREAM OF
  A RIDICULOUS MAN AND SELECTIONS FROM HOUSE OF
  THE DEAD *by Fyodor Dostoyevsky*
  Selected writings by the great Russian author, newly trans-
  lated with an Afterword by Andrew R. MacAndrew.
  (#CP90—60¢)

GIGI and Selected Writings *by Colette*
  Gigi, excerpts from *The Last of Cheri,* and stories, memoirs,
  meditations, and sketches, representing the full scope of
  Colette's genius. Foreword by Elaine Marks.
  (#CT196—75¢)

MCGUFFEY'S SIXTH ECLECTIC READER
  A new edition of a McGuffey Reader, following the popular
  Signet Classic edition of *McGuffey's Fifth Eclectic Reader.*
  Foreword by Henry Steele Commager.   (#CT202—75¢)

BURMESE DAYS *by George Orwell*
  Orwell's first novel presents a scathing indictment of British
  Imperial rule, against a brilliantly rendered exotic back-
  ground. Afterword by Richard Rees.   (#CP194—60¢)

PORTRAIT OF A LADY *by Henry James*
  A probing contrast of American and European mores portrayed through the story of an independent American girl
  who seeks the best of life and love on the Continent. Afterword by Oscar Cargill.   (#CT195—75¢)

THE DEATH OF IVAN ILYCH and Other Stories *by Leo Tolstoy*
  Four stories that probe deeply into the emotions and psy-
  chology of man: *Family Happiness, Master and Man, The
  Kreutzer Sonata,* and the title story. Afterword by David
  Magarshack.   (#CP154—60¢)

THE FALL OF THE HOUSE OF USHER and Other Tales
by Edgar Allan Poe

Masterpieces of the supernatural, by the greatest story writer of all times. With a Foreword by R. P. Blackmur.

(#CD29—50¢)

THE MUTINY ON BOARD H. M. S. BOUNTY *by William Bligh*

The captain's own account of the most famous mutiny to take place in the South Seas. Afterword by Milton Rugoff.

(#CP94—60¢)

BILLY BUDD and Other Tales *by Herman Melville*

The title story and other outstanding short stories, including the *Piazza Tales,* by the author of *Moby Dick.* Afterword by Williard Thorp.

(#CT75—75¢)

ADVENTURES IN THE SKIN TRADE and Other Stories
by Dylan Thomas

Brilliant and fantastic tales by the great Welsh poet, who writes of sinners and lovers, nature and madness. Afterword by Vernon Watkins.

(#CP220—60¢)

ANTON CHEKHOV: SELECTED STORIES

Twenty stories, newly translated by Ann Dunnigan, including a number of early tales which have never before appeared in English. Foreword by Ernest J. Simmons.

(#CP193—60¢)

ADOLPHE AND THE RED NOTE-BOOK *by Benjamin Constant*

By the close friend of Mme. de Stael, this 18th century French novel is the story of a young man's passion for a woman with whom he can never be happy. *Adolphe* translated by Carl Wildman: *The Red Notebook* translated by Norman Cameron. Introduction by Harold Nicolson.

(#CD1—50¢)

THE MARRIAGES and Other Stories *by Henry James*

Nine rarely anthologized stories by the master of sophisticated irony. Foreword by Eleanor M. Tilton.

(#CD87—50¢)